# ESSENTIALS
## of Intellectual Property

# Essentials Series

To keep up with rapid business changes, professionals today need to get up to speed quickly with reliable and clear information. Wiley's Essentials series introduces the first concise guidelines to key topics in finance, accounting, performance improvement, operations, technology, and information management. These books provide in-depth coverage; tips; techniques; and illustrative real-world examples, exhibits, and best practices. The Wiley Essentials series—because the business world is always changing . . . and so should you.

Other books in the series include:

For more information and to receive periodic e-mail notices regarding forthcoming publications, please visit us at *www.wiley.com*.

# ESSENTIALS
## of Intellectual Property

Alexander Poltorak
and
Paul Lerner

JOHN WILEY & SONS, INC.

ISBN: 0-471-20942-2

Printed in the United States of America.

10 9 8 7 6 5 4

# About the Authors

**Alexander I. Poltorak** is the founder and chief executive officer of General Patent Corporation (GPC), an intellectual property (IP) management company focusing on IP strategy, patent licensing and enforcement, international technology transfer, and IP portfolio management. Prior to establishing GPC in 1989, Dr. Poltorak was the president of Poltorak Associates Inc., a management consulting and patent licensing firm, which he formed in 1987. Before that, he was chief executive officer of Rapitech Systems, Inc., a computer company that he co-founded in 1983. Prior to Rapitech, Dr. Poltorak served as Assistant Professor of Biomathematics at the Neurology Department of Cornell University Medical College, where he conducted research in image processing and computer tomography. He also served as Assistant Professor of Physics at Touro College. Dr. Poltorak has published several papers in scientific journals.

Dr. Poltorak emigrated from the former USSR in 1982, where he was awarded a doctorate in physics at the age of 22 for a significant breakthrough in Einstein's Theory of Relativity. As a political dissident, he was later stripped of his degrees for anticommunist activities. He is a member of the Licensing Executives Society (LES), the Association of University Technology Managers (AUTM), Intellectual Property Owners Association (IPO), the National Association of Corporate Directors, the New York Academy of Science, and the American Physical Society. He was a U.S. co-chairman for the Subcommittee on Information Exchange of the US-USSR Trade and Economic Counsel. He is on the advisory board of *Patent Strategy & Management*, for which he co-wrote "Corporate Officers and Directors Can Be Liable for

Mismanaging Intellectual Property." The article appeared in its May and June 2000 issues. He is co-author with Paul Lerner of an article about *Grain Processing v. American Maize Products,* "Grain, Grain, Go Away," which examines recent major developments in patent infringement damages. The article appeared in the February 2000 edition of *Intellectual Property Worldwide.*

**Paul J. Lerner** is the Senior Vice President and General Counsel of General Patent Corporation (GPC). Before joining GPC, Mr. Lerner was a partner in the Hartford, Connecticut, business law firm of Pepe & Hazard LLP. He has led IP law departments at Olin Corporation, Black & Decker Corporation, and multinational electrical construction giant Asea Brown Boveri, Inc.

Prior to embarking on a law career, Mr. Lerner was a project manager at the Illinois Institute of Technology Research Institute in Chicago, where he managed a technology transfer and technology forecasting team. Mr. Lerner's education includes a BS in Aeronautical Engineering from Purdue University, an MBA from Loyola University, a JD from DePaul University, and postgraduate legal studies at John Marshall College of Law. He is an Adjunct Professor of IP law at the University of New Haven.

Mr. Lerner is a member of the Licensing Executives Society (LES) and the American Intellectual Property Law Association (AIPLA). He is co-author with GPC's chairman and CEO, Alexander Poltorak, of an article about *Grain processing v. American Maize Products,* "Grain, Grain, Go Away." He also co-wrote "Corporate Officers and Directors Can Be Liable for Mismanaging Intellectual Property." In September 2000, Mr. Lerner's article "Strategic Auditing: The Key to Minimizing Litigation Bills" was published by *corporateintelligence.com.*

General Patent Corporation is based in Montebello Park, Suffern, New York.

# Contents

# Foreword

As I write this, the U.S. Patent and Trademark Office has just released its annual report of the top ten private sector organizations receiving patents in the prior year. A comparison of the listing for 2001 to those of past years reveals that the number of patents required to rank first (as IBM has done since 1993) has more than tripled in the past decade; the total number of U.S. patents issued annually has gone up nearly sixty-five percent; and the proportion garnered by the top ten–all well known electronics companies—has increased from seven and one-half percent to nearly ten percent of all patents issued in 2001.

Fascinating statistics, but what's behind them? Simply put, it's money. Dollars, Yen, Euros, billions of them collected in the form of royalties every year by companies and individuals (the late Jerome Lemelson, for example) with valuable intellectual property, principally patents. IBM alone will have received nearly two billion dollars during 2001 in IP-related payments, most of it cash, and nearly all of it pure profit. Canon, Hitachi, Lucent and many other top patent holders enjoy significant returns on their R&D investments. And then there are the software companies, Oracle, Microsoft and, yes, IBM again, whose products **are** intellectual property, protected globally by copyrights and earning billions in sales.

No wonder companies of all sizes throughout the world (eight of the USPTO's top ten are non-U.S. companies) are paying close attention to acquiring and leveraging patents, copyrights, trademarks and other intellectual property. What was once the province of the patent department, all too often a corporate backwater, now has the full attention of most CFOs and many CEOs. As IP is seldom taught outside of law schools, and then only to those focused on this niche of jurisprudence, where can the business executive turn for a clear, concise and useful briefing on this new phenomena? Most legal tomes cover in dreary prose, and at great length, every aspect of IP law, but none of the exciting potential of their subject matter. ESSENTIALS OF INTELLECTUAL PROPERTY, by Alexander Poltorak and Paul Lerner, admirably fills this vacuum.

The authors—who are the principals of General Patent Corporation, an imaginative and successful intellectual property management and licensing firm—not only know the subject matter, they explore the nuances, and expose the pitfalls, in a thorough and refreshingly readable fashion. They resort to plain English to guide us to a clear understanding of "the currency of the New Economy" by systematically explaining the essential legal elements and business value of each type of IP, with useful suggestions of how to acquire, protect and deploy these fruits of creativity.

It is well realized that most IP, particularly that held by corporations, is undervalued and unappreciated. As IP is usually not reflected on the balance sheet (there is currently a groundswell of proposals to change this), it is widely ignored by those charged with providing a return on investment, as represented by assets. On the other hand, the returns are extremely generous once these valuable assets are recognized and tapped for their potential. The authors provide comprehensive and useful insight and guidance for an effective process of protection, recognition, valuation and exploitation of what a recent book on the subject referred to as "Rembrandts in the Attic" (Kevin G. Rivette and David Kline, *Rembrandts in the Attic* [Boston: Harvard School Press, 1999]).

A chapter addressing the prospect of liability to corporate executives and directors for mismanaging intellectual property makes sobering reading, and if nothing else will, should be a wake-up call to many who have approved large sums to acquire IP without having a clue of what to do with it, and why. If this were not sufficient, the final chapter "The Patent Portfolio And Its Effect On Stock Price" should arouse the most somnolent of corporate custodians.

Poltorak and Lerner have provided a clear and useful road map for the non-lawyer business executive, without stinting on necessary detail, and surprisingly for the genre, have done so with much grace and good humor. Moreover, the Appendices include very usable sample forms which address everything from applying for a patent to a model license agreement.

I can think of no more sincere tribute to Alex and Paul than to say "This is the book I wish I had written."

Emmett J. Murtha
Stamford, CT
January 25, 2002

# Preface

## Intellectual Property—The Currency of the New Economy

Intellectual property, also known simply as IP, has become one of the most talked about topics in business today, yet it is still one of the least understood. Simply stated, intellectual property consists of products of the human mind and creativity that are protected by law. It is an intangible, lacking physical substance. It has neither length nor width nor height. It has no weight and casts no shadow. It is colorless, odorless, and tasteless.

Like tangible property, intellectual property can be bought, sold, and rented. Also like tangible property, it can be lost or destroyed through carelessness or neglect. It is insurable and could be used as a collateral. It may be the result of a momentary flash of inspiration or years of diligent and painstaking labor. It may be lost in a moment or continue in perpetuity.

Whatever its other characteristics, however, intellectual property *does* have economic value—often, great economic value—although this value is often overlooked, underestimated, and underreported. In business, it may constitute either an opportunity or a threat, depending (in large part) on who owns it.

It has often been said that "knowledge is power." Although unsaid, knowledge is also wealth. Indeed, in today's knowledge-based economy, intellectual property is often the single most important asset of an enterprise. Intangible assets now represent almost 75% of the total market value of the Standard and Poor's (S&P) 500 companies, double what it was 10 years ago.

Those companies that fail to accord intellectual property a position at the top of the corporate agenda are now, at best, doomed to lose competitive advantage; at worst, they may face ruin. It is for this reason that businesspeople should have a basic understanding of the nature and uses of intellectual property.

Intellectual property presents different opportunities (and different challenges) as an enterprise or an industry moves through the normal business life cycle. It may constitute the basis for a start-up company, or even a new industry. It may offer new products or services to growing enterprises; and, in mature industries, it may comprise the competitive advantage that spells the difference between prosperity or decline and ultimate demise.

Until recently, it was thought that intellectual property was of concern only to a rare few engineers and scientists (and, of course, to the patent attorneys). This belief, never correct, is now largely discredited. In actuality, intellectual property is, or properly should be, of concern to marketing and product planning staffs, engineers and product designers, and product promotion and advertising personnel. Needless to say, intellectual property must be well understood and be of foremost concern to the corporate boards, chief executive officers (CEOs), chief financial officers (CFOs), entrepreneurs, and other business managers. Indeed, with the advent and subsequent explosion in business method patents, there are now few, if any, business functions that need not concern themselves with intellectual property. In addition, the courts are increasingly recognizing the duty of care owed by corporate officers and directors in the management (i.e., the protection, effective utilization, and proper valuation) of a firm's intellectual property.

In the Introduction to this book, intellectual property is defined and its uses described. The reader is then introduced, in Chapters 1 and 2, to the various types of IP, and how they can be protected.

The book next addresses the management of intellectual property. Chapters are devoted to documenting inventions and IP portfolio management (Chapter 3) and gathering and using competitive intelligence (Chapter 4). Chapter 5 identifies various approaches to the valuation of intellectual property, and Chapter 6 discusses ways in which this value may be realized.

Chapter 7 addresses the responsibilities of the business manager with respect to IP, and presents guidelines as to how these responsibilities can be satisfied.

In Chapter 8, the key issues involved in IP enforcement are presented and analyzed, namely: development of an enforcement strategy, law firm selection and management, costs, risks, and litigation risk analysis.

Finally, Chapter 9 addresses the IP problems created by cyberspace and e-commerce, and Chapter 10 deals with the effects that patent portfolios may have on stock price.

# Author's Note

It is the purpose of this book to introduce the business executive to the principles underlying the identification, protection, and use of intellectual property in the business environment. To this end, key concepts and facts have been described, and the authors have attempted to illustrate how these concepts and facts influence (actually, should influence) decision making, from the formulation of routine procedures to strategic planning. Of necessity, these descriptions are generalized.

Exceptions abound to every rule stated in the following chapters (your lawyer will, no doubt, be more than happy to enumerate these exceptions for you). Moreover, the law is a living, constantly evolving creature. The rules of the game are constantly changing—often in midplay and sometimes retroactively. A little knowledge is a dangerous thing. Before proceeding, review matters with a qualified professional. Reading this book, however carefully, is no substitute for professional guidance.

# Acknowledgments

The authors wish to express their gratitude to Samson Vermont, who has graciously provided much of the patent statistics cited in this book.

Our editors, Susan McDermott, Jennifer Gaines, and others at John Wiley & Sons, deserve much thanks for seeing this work through.

Kim Gill, Kathy Ingham, and Valeria Poltorak provided valuable assistance.

Without the tireless efforts and unfailing good cheer of Naava Cooper, this work would not have been completed.

While the credit goes to many who have assisted us, the errors are all ours.

# Introduction: Setting the Stage

## Intellectual Capital, Intellectual Assets, and Intellectual Property

Intellectual property has become a *cliché de jour* of the business world. That intellectual property is important is also evidenced by the fact that, of late, everyone is trying to get into the act. Formerly, only patent attorneys used the word *intellectual* as in *intellectual property*. Now, however, we have management consultants speaking of *intellectual capital*, while accountants and economists write about *intellectual assets*. Nevertheless, the concepts underlying these terms have significance, and it would be well to understand them.

### Intellectual Capital: What They Thought Up

Intellectual capital, in its simplest sense, comprises the sum total of all knowledge in an enterprise. It is what everyone in a firm knows, and what therefore gives the firm its competitive advantage. Intellectual capital includes the knowledge and skills of employees; the processes, ideas, designs, inventions, and technologies utilized by the firm; and the relationships it has developed with both customers and suppliers. It includes software, business methods, manuals, reports, publications, and databases. It includes not only knowledge and information, but also the intangible infrastructure that facilitates its use, exchange, and retention. Needless to say, intellectual capital includes patents, trademarks, copyrights, trade dress rights, Internet domain names, and the like.

**TIPS & TECHNIQUES**

Intellectual capital is the sum total of all knowledge in an enterprise, as it resides in the minds of its employees, which can be leveraged to create wealth.

In the broadest sense, intellectual capital is what is left of an enterprise after it has been stripped of all its tangible assets, such as land, buildings, machinery, inventory, and cash.

**Intellectual Capital = enterprise value − value of all hard assets**

Intellectual capital cannot exist outside the context of a particular enterprise or independent of its strategy. Intellectual capital, which may be at the heart of one business, may be utterly useless to another business. Moreover, it is only a clearly defined strategy that can separate useful knowledge from informational noise and disparate facts. It is the structure imposed by a strategy that brings order and meaning to what is otherwise informational chaos. Like a magnet attracts iron filings, strategy and purpose create the discernable informational patterns that we call knowledge.

**Purpose → Strategy → Information → Knowledge**

## Intellectual Assets: What They Wrote Down

While intellectual capital is the cornerstone of the modern business enterprise, much of it is tacit knowledge that resides in the minds of its employees. When an employee leaves the organization, so does the intellectual capital that resides in the employee—the employee's know-

**TIPS & TECHNIQUES**

Intellectual assets are intellectual capital that is identified, documented, and available to be shared and replicated within the organization.

ledge, experience, skills, creativity, and relations with others (customers, suppliers, and other employees). Stated succinctly, intellectual capital is what walks out the door at the end of the day. Obviously, there is a risk that it won't walk back in tomorrow. Moreover, even while an employee is working for an organization, his or her knowledge cannot be most effectively utilized unless it is identified, documented, and shared with others. Thus, the principal objectives of intellectual capital management are to identify, capture, and document it and to make it accessible to others in the organization. Intellectual capital that has been so captured, preserved, catalogued, and made available for sharing is known as *intellectual assets.*

An organization does not own its employees—they can leave or may be fired. But the organization does own the intellectual assets they create while a part of the organization. Clearly, it is in the best interest of the business enterprise to encourage its employees to disclose and record this intellectual capital (programs to achieve this goal are discussed and described in Chapter 3).

Intellectual Capital Management Process Flow:

**Search out → Identify → Capture → Document →
Index → Store → Augment → Replicate**

## Intellectual Property: What You Protected

Intellectual assets legally protected under applicable laws are called *intellectual property.* A typical example of intellectual property is a patent that is protected by the patent law (Title 35 of the United States Code).

Intellectual capital, intellectual assets, and intellectual property overlap (see Exhibit I.1). Intellectual assets form a more valuable subset of intellectual capital, and intellectual property forms an even more valuable subset of intellectual assets. The growth in value dictates the flow of the management process: to distill intellectual assets from intellectual capital and to further distill intellectual property from intellectual assets. Thus, it is the goal of management to produce intellectual property.

The broad spectrum of intellectual property may be divided into two segments: the (supposedly) well-defined "classical" or statutory assets and the less definite contractual or "common law" assets (although

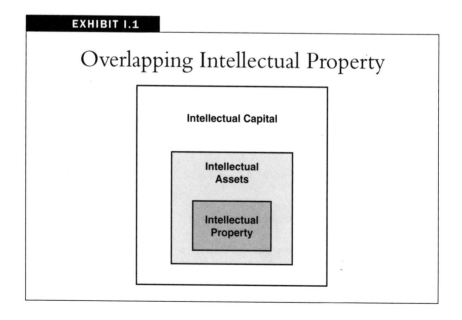

**EXHIBIT I.1**

# Overlapping Intellectual Property

**Intellectual Capital**

**Intellectual Assets**

**Intellectual Property**

**TIPS & TECHNIQUES**

Intellectual property is intellectual assets that are protected under applicable laws.

these too may be governed by statute—generally, but not exclusively, state statutes). The former segment comprises the well-known, but often misunderstood, trinity of patents, trademarks, and copyrights and, in recent years, has expanded to include mask works and registered designs. The latter segment comprises trade secrets and know-how, as well as noncompetition agreements and confidential disclosure agreements.

# CHAPTER 1

# The Big Three: Patents, Trademarks, and Copyrights

 **After reading this chapter you will be able to:**

- Understand the various kinds of patents and the nature of the protection offered by each

- Understand what constitutes patent infringement

- Understand the major considerations and factors to be borne in mind when securing patents

- Know the factors involved in choosing a good patent attorney

- Understand the nature of trademarks and service marks and the requirements for registration of these marks, as well as the proper mode of use of a trademark or service mark

- Know how to choose a mark and determine whether it is available for adoption

- Understand the nature of copyrights along with the uses of copyrights in nontraditional applications, such as protection of computer software

- Recognize "work for hire" situations that may call for a written copyright assignment

- Understand the Doctrine of Fair Use

# Patents

A patent conveys to its owner the right to prevent others from making, using, selling, offering for sale (this last is a recent addition), or importing the patented invention. Patents are national in nature, having effect only within the territory of the issuing country.

The patent law of the United States provides for three kinds of patents: plant patents, design patents, and utility patents. Plant patents cover asexually reproduced plants and are primarily of interest only to plant breeders. Design patents cover the ornamental design of an article (i.e., its appearance) to the extent that that design or appearance is dictated by aesthetic, rather than functional, considerations. The majority of patents are of the third kind—utility patents—and it is with these that we shall be mostly, but not exclusively, concerned.

A utility patent, generally speaking, may cover a device or an article, a composition of matter, a method or a process of doing or making something, or, less commonly, a new application for an existing device or material, or a product (otherwise known and, therefore, not patentable) made by a particular new process.

In order to qualify for a patent, an invention must be novel, nonobvious, and useful. The utility requirement is largely self-explanatory

**IN THE REAL WORLD**

## The Constitutional Basis of Our Patent Laws

"The Congress shall have the power to promote the progress of Science and useful Arts, by Securing for a Limited Time to Authors and Inventors the exclusive Right to their respective Writings and Discoveries." —the U.S. Constitution, Article I, Section 8

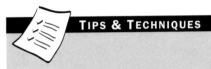

**TIPS & TECHNIQUES**

To be patentable, an invention must be:

- Novel

- Nonobvious

- Useful

and rarely comprises a significant obstacle to patentability. If the invention works, it has utility. A new chemical compound may not be patentable in and of itself, unless there is a useful application for it. The requirement of novelty is satisfied if no single prior art reference discloses all of the features of the invention (i.e., the same invention was not made earlier by someone else). The most challenging, and conceptually most complex, requirement for patentability is nonobviousness. To satisfy this last requirement, the invention must not be merely a combination of elements of prior works, such as would be apparent to a person of "ordinary skill in the art" who was seeking to solve the problem to which the invention is directed.

Formerly, a United States utility patent had a term of 17 years, commencing on the patent's issue date. Under the current law, however, utility patents have a term of 20 years, commencing on the date of filing of the application on which it is based. The new law applies to patents issuing on applications filed on or after June 8, 1995. Patents issued on earlier filed applications now have a term of either 17 years from the date of issue or 20 years from the date of filing, whichever is longer. Although, in theory, the term of a patent may be extended if its prosecution is unduly delayed by the Patent Office, as a practical matter, a patent term is nonextendable. The primary exception is for those patents directed to pharmaceutical products, in which case the term may be extended to compensate for time lost in securing the applicable regulatory (Food and Drug Administration) approval. Design patents have a term of 14 years from date of issue.

As a result of statutory requirements, and rules promulgated by the United States Patent and Trademark Office (USPTO), the format and content of utility patents is relatively standardized. Preceding the textual portions of the patent are one or more pages of drawings of the "preferred embodiment" of the invention (for all intents and purposes, *preferred embodiment* is synonymous with *best mode*—see the section "What You Don't Tell" later in the chapter for more on this fascinating topic). The patent text begins with a brief statement identifying the subject of the invention. A background section that states the problem that is solved by the invention follows this. This statement of the problem may include a description of prior solutions or attempted solutions and the reasons why they were not wholly satisfactory. Following the background section is a section summarizing the invention, including its key features and advantages. Next is a section providing a brief description of the patent drawings, specifying what is being illustrated in each figure. Following this is a rather lengthy section setting forth a detailed description of the invention with reference to the preferred embodiment illustrated in the drawings. These textual portions of the patent are known as the specification. Finally, the patent concludes with the patent claims, which are the consecutively numbered sentences at the end of the patent document. Preceding the patent is a cover sheet, which includes a brief abstract and a wealth of other useful information that will be described in a later chapter.

## What to Be Concerned About

Few members of the general public have much knowledge about patents. Moreover, much of what is commonly believed about patents is incorrect. Perhaps the most common misconception is that a patent gives its owner the right to practice the patented invention. As noted above, a patent conveys the right to prevent others from practicing the patented invention—an exclusionary or negative right. It does *not* convey an affirmative or positive right to the patent owner to practice the patented invention. The difference between the two types of rights—exclusionary or negative and affirmative or positive—is best (and most often) seen in the context of an "improvement patent" that covers an improvement to an existing article or process which is, itself, covered by an unexpired patent. If, as is frequently the case, practice of the improvement necessitates making the underlying basic or unimproved article, or performing the basic process, the holder of the patent on the unimproved article or process can prevent such practice. In these circumstances, the owner of the improvement patent cannot practice his or her own patented invention. This concept can best be understood with reference to the following hypothetical situation, which will be used for illustrative purposes throughout this book.

Suppose there is no such thing as a fire engine. (This *is* a hypothetical situation and we wish to avoid adding technological complexity to the matter.) Jack lives in a rural area of largely wooden houses that lacks a municipal water system. Lack of a ready supply of water makes combating a fire in one of these houses difficult. Perceiving this problem, Jack proceeds to invent and patent (a utility patent) a fire engine, which comprises a vehicle bearing a tank of water, a pump, and a hose and nozzle (for the moment, we need not concern ourselves with a more specific definition of *fire engine*).

One fine day Jill happens upon a fire engine, on its way to a fire, caught in traffic. Jill perceives that delays caused by traffic are a problem in that they interfere with prompt firefighting efforts. Jill concludes that this problem would be solved, or at least ameliorated, if other motorists could be made aware of the nature of the fire engine and its mission, namely that it is an emergency vehicle on an emergency mission. Jill determines that such awareness could best be achieved by painting the fire engine a distinctive color (red) and providing it with both visual and auditory warning devices (a flashing red light and a bell). Jill proceeds to patent (again, a utility patent) this improved fire engine, which comprises a fire engine painted red and bearing a flashing red light and a bell.

Under the circumstances of our hypothetical situation, would Jill have the right to make, use, sell, or offer for sale improved fire engines as set forth in her patent (red fire engines with flashing red lights and bells)? The answer to this question is "no." In order to make an improved fire engine, Jill must also make a fire engine; and Jack, by reason of his patent, would have the right to prevent Jill from doing so. However, Jack cannot make or use an improved version of his fire engine (red paint, flashing light, and bell) because Jill, by reason of her patent, has the right to prevent this. (Cross-licensing often breaks such impasses.)

Another point of misunderstanding with respect to patents is what they cover. Inventors are often a veritable font of misinformation in this regard, speaking broadly (and grandiloquently) about "my invention" or "my basic invention" or—even worse—"my concept," while belittling any minor changes or minor variations made by an accused infringer. *Do not listen to such people.* What a patent covers is determined by its claims. While the claims are to be "construed" (i.e., interpreted) in light of the patent specification, it is the claims that determine what the patent covers (more on this subject shortly).

Similarly, technical people, when requested to review a patent (especially after the reviewer's employer has been charged with infringing that patent), will often read the abstract and the summary of the invention, look at the drawings, and opine that the patent is invalid because "it's all old" or "we've been doing that for years." *Do not listen to such people.* Most inventions are improvements on some earlier technology, and most inventions are described in the context of the environment in which they are intended to function. As a result, much of what appears in the patent drawings and is described in the patent specification is old. However, the scope of a patent is determined by its claims. (We are repeating this point because it merits repetition. It is often overlooked, occasionally even by judges.) A patent examiner, before allowing (approving) the patent, found some limitation in the claims of the patent that, in his (mostly) expert opinion, constituted a legal basis of patentability. This basis can generally be discerned by an examination of the file wrapper of the patent, which is a publicly available copy of all of the documents relating to the issuance of the patent. Never accept any opinion as to patent validity or scope that is not based on a thorough review of the patent file wrapper by a patent attorney (the courts won't, when it comes to a question of willful infringement).

## What You Don't Know

It is often said, "What you don't know won't hurt you." This does not apply in business. It equally does not apply with respect to patents. Patent infringement is not a specific intent tort—in layman's terms, that means that one may infringe a patent without intending to do so. Patent infringement may be innocent, but it is patent infringement nonetheless. It is not a defense to a charge of patent infringement that you were unaware of the allegedly infringed patent (although, as we will see, it

**TIPS & TECHNIQUES**

Unintentional infringement is infringement nonetheless.

may mitigate the damages). It is therefore highly advisable to perform a product clearance patent search before marketing a new product or utilizing a new production process. Indeed, such a search should preferably precede any substantial new product or process investment or development effort.

## What You Don't Tell

In addition to questions of patent infringement, there are several basic, but not commonly known, requirements for a patent that, if ignored, may result in the invalidity of any patent thereafter obtained.

A patent must be enabling and it must include a disclosure of the best mode of practicing the claimed invention. In essence, this means that, based on the patent document, a hypothetical (actually mythical) person of "ordinary skill in the art" (a term that appears frequently in patent matters) must be able to practice the patented invention with only a *reasonable* amount of experimentation; and that where there is more than one way to practice the patented invention, the patentee has disclosed what he or she considers, at the time of filing of the patent application, to be the best way to practice it, known as the *best mode*. Thus, it is vitally important when disclosing an invention to a patent attorney who will draft a patent application that nothing be withheld or concealed. A choice must be made between maintaining a trade secret and obtaining a patent with respect to an invention. Such choices may be difficult. However, if you try to have both, you may wind up with neither. *Do not try to beat the system.* A patent examiner, when examining a patent application, will not challenge, but will accept, the disclosed embodiment of the invention as being the best mode, and may not notice a missing detail that defeats enablement. Opposing counsel, in litigation, will challenge everything and will likely have almost unlimited resources, including discovery procedures, available. Expect that opposing counsel will miss nothing. Any victory gained by concealing information is likely to be only temporary.

Another frequently (or conveniently) overlooked or unconsidered aspect of patent law pertains to what are described as *statutory bars*. Simply stated, the law requires that an inventor make a reasonably prompt decision as to whether to seek patent protection for an invention. The need to make this decision is triggered by public disclosure of the invention, or by the first sale, or first offer for sale, of articles made in accord with the invention—even if no sale is actually effected.

Once such an event has occurred, a patent application must be filed —actually received by the USPTO—within one year, or the law bars patent protection for the invention. The courts strictly enforce this requirement. The one-year period, known as a grace period, is virtually unique to the United States. Other countries essentially require that a patent application be filed before disclosure or sale of the invention (the so-called strict novelty requirement). Therefore, if foreign patent protection is desired, action should be taken to file a U.S. patent application before marketing efforts begin or other public disclosure is made.

## What You Don't Disclose

Among the burdens placed on a patent applicant and the applicant's patent attorney (if any—see the following section of this chapter) is the duty of candor, also known as the duty of disclosure.

Patent examiners have limited time and limited resources with which to search for relevant prior art. In order to aid the examiner in identifying such art, thereby preventing the grant of invalid patents, each individual associated with the filing and prosecution of a patent application is impressed with the duty to disclose to the Patent Office all material "known to that individual to be material to patentability." If such an individual fails to satisfy this obligation—withholding known prior art

**TIPS & TECHNIQUES**

Do not conceal prior art—it will come back to haunt you!

from the Patent Office—such failure, known as inequitable conduct (formerly known as "fraud on the Patent Office") may result in a patent's being found invalid or unenforceable.

There are those who would point out that, if the patent applicant does not disclose a prior art reference, it is quite possible that it will not be discovered by the patent examiner. Further, even if the examiner *does* discover the reference, no harm will be suffered. The examiner will not inquire as to possible failure to disclose, but will merely proceed with examination of the application. The implied advice therefore is to forget any information that might imperil the grant of a patent. *Do not listen to such people.* Apart from the ethical considerations, there always exists the possibility that the patent will become the subject of litigation. While the patent examiner was handicapped in searching for prior art, opposing counsel will enjoy substantial, if not virtually limitless, resources. Moreover, opposing counsel has recourse to discovery procedures once litigation commences. Files and records can be examined, and witnesses can be deposed. Thus, the "forgotten" reference may well be discovered. Mere discovery is bad enough. If it is also established that the patent applicant was aware of the reference but failed to disclose it to the Patent Office, *real* trouble may ensue. For example, seeking to enforce a patent known to be invalid may comprise a violation of the antitrust laws. Therefore, do not conceal references from your patent attorney, and do not ask your patent attorney to conceal references from the Patent Office. (Although sometimes tedious, patent attorneys are, as a group, highly ethical.)

## Design Patents—Where Less Is More

It is commonly believed (even by some patent attorneys, who should know better) that design patents are very limited in scope and, hence, are of little value, except to prevent exact copying of specific product designs. *Do not listen to such people.* Design patents, in actuality, occupy a significant—if not stellar—position in the intellectual property universe.

Because applications for design patents are, both in principle and in execution, quite simple, attorneys often give them short shrift; indeed, they are most often prepared by paralegals (whereby they yield a significant profit margin to the law firm). Drawings or photographs of the subject product, provided by the client, are simply attached to a largely boilerplate application and filed in the Patent Office. Patents issuing on such applications will, in fact, protect the depicted product design and little, if anything, else. If the scope of such patents is found wanting, however, the fault lies not in the inherent nature of design patents, but in the lack of effort on the part of those who prepared the applications.

Drawings utilized in design patent applications should be "cleaned up"—unnecessary design details should be deleted. The more basic the design is, the more difficult it is to circumvent.

More importantly (and less widely known), a patented design need not encompass an entire "article of manufacture." In a landmark decision (*In Re Zahn,* 617 F.2d 261, 204 USPQ 988 [CCPA 1980])—a case brilliantly briefed and argued by one of the authors of this book—the Court of Customs and Patent Appeals (the predecessor to the Court of Appeals for the Federal Circuit, also known as the "Patent Court") held that a patented design must pertain to a complete article, but that the design need not encompass the entire article. Thus, it is possible to patent a design of a *portion* of a product, whereby the appearance of the remaining portion, which does not bear the patented design, is irrelevant to the question of patent infringement. Such a design patent may be quite broad in scope. No manufacturer should ignore design patents.

## Provisional Patent Applications—When You Care Enough to Send the Second Best

Provisional patent applications are, essentially, utility or conventional patent applications from which the claims have been omitted. They may be viewed as merely an optional, preliminary step in the process of securing a utility patent. The filing of a provisional patent application must be followed, within one year, by the filing of a utility patent application. Failure to do so results in the irreversible abandonment of the provisional application.

When first introduced in 1995, the provisional patent application was touted as a low-cost means of establishing a patent application priority date while simultaneously offering the inventor a period of time (one year) to further develop and refine the invention and to decide whether to undertake the costly filing and prosecution of a regular patent application. A further benefit, ostensibly, is derived from the fact that the term of pendency of a provisional patent application is not included in the 20-year term of a patent. Thus, the provisional patent application, in effect, offered a means of extending the life of a patent by up to a year.

These acclaimed advantages have proven largely illusory, for the simple reason that a provisional patent application is, after all, a patent application, and is subject to the same disclosure requirements as a utility patent application—it must be enabling and it must teach each and every limitation that will appear in the claims of the corresponding future utility patent application (it must provide support for the claims). Indeed, if done properly, a provisional patent application is virtually identical to the specification of the corresponding utility patent application. Thus, while the filing fee for a provisional patent application is considerably less than the filing fee for the corresponding utility patent application, the cost of *drafting* the provisional application is a considerable fraction of the cost of drafting a utility application. The total cost savings therefore is nowhere near as significant as some people believe. Moreover, if the further development and refinement of the invention results in technological changes or details not described in the provisional application (how could they be described if they were created after the filing?), such new developments do not receive the benefit of the filing date of the provisional application. Incorporation of these developments into the utility patent application generally requires the filing of a continuation-in-part application, thus adding further costs.

Finally, there is a serious question as to the value of any patent term extension achieved by the use of provisional patent applications. With the present rapid technological advances, most patented inventions are obsolete long before the patent expires. (Electronics inventions are, on average, obsolete within three to five years of the issuance of the patent.) Thus, it may be much more advantageous to speed the issue of a patent than to delay its expiration. The real advantage of provisional patent applications (if any) may lie in combating the pernicious effects of the *Festo* decision (see Chapter 8).

Some inventors (and, embarrassingly, some patent attorneys) will advocate filing all sorts of technical papers, research reports, and interim project specifications as provisional patent applications. *Do not listen to such people.* Such documents, without revision, invariably lack the level of detail and completeness necessary to support a future utility patent application.

There are, of course, the rare exceptions to this rule. When one is a day short of expiration of the one-year grace period (which has been triggered by publication of a research paper or sale of the product), one may have no choice but to quickly file the provisional application to prevent "crossing the bar." Finally, in certain instances it may be beneficial to delay commencement of the patent term by a year (the protection will commence and expire a year later). Even though one will not gain an extra year of patent life, as often thought, one will push the patent term one year forward. In no event should one consider drafting a provisional patent application *pro se*—by oneself. Only in cases of extreme emergency should such practice be allowed. If a development has potential value, and the inventor wishes to file a provisional patent application while considering the matter further, the application should be prepared by a competent professional.

## Choosing a Patent Attorney

Accused criminals have the legal right to represent themselves in court. It is widely acknowledged, however, that one who does so has a fool for a client. Similarly, inventors have the legal right to represent themselves in the Patent Office and, similarly, one who does so has a fool for a client.

Patents are not all equal in the eyes of the law. Some afford broad protection and, hence, are of great value. Others are very narrow in scope and are, therefore, easily circumvented. These are, obviously, of little value. The quality (and value) of a patent is highly dependent on the skill and knowledge of the person who drafts and prosecutes the patent application. Expertise in both the relevant technology and patent law and procedure are required. Such expertise is not inexpensive. However, as the old saying goes, "If something is worth doing, it's worth doing well." In business terms, the incremental costs of properly drafting and prosecuting a patent application are more than adequately compensated by the incremental value of the patent thus obtained.

It must be borne in mind that the starting point in the preparation of a patent application is a blank sheet of paper (or a blank word processor screen). Drafting a patent application is not a matter of filling in blank spaces in a form. Each patent application is an individually crafted work of art (as noted above, depending on the draftsperson—some are more artful than others). Just as no two inventions are alike, so too no two patent applications are alike. For this reason, patent practitioners almost always bill for prosecution services by the hour. The chief exception to this general rule occurs when a client has a substantial number of patent applications to be prepared. In such cases, a law firm may quote a fixed price per application, relying on the law of averages—some applications will be relatively complex (and time consuming), while others will be comparatively simple (and quickly completed).

Many inventors, or business managers, search long and hard to find the patent practitioner with the lowest billing rate. *Do not do this*. More often than not, an unusually low billing rate connotes a lack of experience or skill, or both. Moreover, the final cost of an application is the hourly billing rate of the draftsperson, multiplied by the number of hours billed. An inexperienced or inefficient practitioner, with a comparatively low billing rate, often requires more time to complete an application than a more experienced colleague with a higher hourly rate. Because of the variability in the amount of time billed, there is often little correlation between the hourly billing rate and the cost of the completed patent application. Indeed, the more experienced practitioner may actually prove less costly. If price comparison is absolutely

**TIPS & TECHNIQUES**

Trying to save money on a patent attorney is akin to shopping for the cheapest brain surgeon.

necessary, ask the various candidate practitioners to estimate the cost to draft an application in respect of a specimen invention disclosure.

A factor frequently overlooked when selecting a patent practitioner is the individual's technical background. Patent attorneys and patent agents are, of necessity, quick studies and are generally able to work with inventions in a broad spectrum of technologies. Nevertheless, all other things being equal, it is preferable, in terms of both cost and quality, to secure the services of a practitioner with prior experience in the field of technology to which the invention pertains. Moreover, there are some types of inventions, for example, pharmaceutical and bioengineering inventions, that should be handled only by practitioners with the corresponding technical education. Inquire as to a prospect's technical background (education and experience) when making your choice.

## A Good Attorney or Another Engineer

Having noted that a patent attorney should have appropriate technical expertise, it must also be borne in mind that a patent is a legal document, the proper drafting of which requires *legal* expertise. Over the past several years, a trend has developed toward ever-increasing levels of technical education among those patent attorneys engaging primarily, if not exclusively, in patent prosecution. This trend is even more pronounced among patent agents. Thus, more and more often one finds patent practitioners with master's degrees or doctorate degrees in technical fields. Some even boast of postdoctoral studies (apparently, they entered the patent field only when spouses or mothers insisted they finally get a job).

To an extent, this trend may be driven by the increasing complexity of some of the technologies now being patented; and to this extent the trend may be beneficial. To a much greater extent, however, the trend results from one of the most common of management flaws—the undue attention and preference accorded the familiar and the avoidance of the unfamiliar. Most often, patent practitioners report to a senior member of the client's engineering staff. Such staff members, themselves technologically oriented, with little or no legal knowledge, often prefer patent practitioners who focus on (and talk about) technological rather than legal issues. When retaining patent counsel, make certain to retain a legal advisor, not to hire an addition to the engineering department.

The alert reader will have noticed the use of the term *patent agent*. A patent agent is a person who has passed the Patent Office Bar Examination. Such a person is entitled to practice in the Patent Office, preparing so-called patentability opinions (more on this exciting document follows shortly) and filing and prosecuting patent applications. A patent attorney, however, has passed the patent bar and is also an attorney admitted to the bar of one of the 50 states or the District of Columbia. Those activities deemed to constitute the practice of law— rendering patent validity or infringement opinions, engaging in litigation, or drafting license documents—may be performed only by a lawyer, not by a patent agent.

## The Process of Obtaining a Patent

Before the drafting of a patent application has commenced, one may request, or the practitioner may recommend, that a patent search be performed. Also known as a novelty search, patentability search, or prior art search, this involves searching through the relevant prior art—principally, but not always exclusively, the collection of prior patents and published articles and brochures maintained by the Patent Office—to identify that art which is pertinent to the patentability (novelty and nonobviousness) of the subject invention. While the law does not require such a search, it is almost always a wise measure. Occasionally, such a search will reveal that the invention in question is not patentable —it lacks novelty ("it's been done before"), or it is obvious in view of the prior art. Such a revelation, while discouraging, at least results in a savings of the cost of the patent application that would otherwise have been drafted and filed.

Much more frequently, however, the search results enable the patent practitioner to better identify patentable aspects or features of the invention and to focus the patent application on these features. After a patent application has been filed, no "new matter" may be added to the drawings or the specification—they are essentially frozen when the patent application is filed. While the claims may be (and most often are) amended during the prosecution of the application, they cannot cover anything that is not shown in the drawings and described in the specification. Thus, there is great value to foreknowledge ("forewarned is forearmed") such as may be gained through a patent search.

Indeed, a patentability search is becoming almost mandatory in view of the recent *Festo* decision (more on this later). In essence, the *Festo* decision affixes a steep price to any claim amendment that changes the scope of a claim in order to avoid reading on the prior art. This price is complete loss of the range of equivalents, which would otherwise be available to the patentee under the Doctrine of Equivalents (a topic discussed more fully in Chapter 8). Unless and until the Supreme Court (which has accepted the case) overturns the *Festo* decision, it will be highly advisable to do a patentability search in order to enable drafting of the patent claims in such a manner that they need not be amended later.

Anywhere from 7 to 23 months after an application is filed, depending on the field of technology to which it pertains and the backlog in that particular section ("Art Group") of the Patent Office, a written report known as an "Official Office Action" is issued. In this office action, the patent examiner identifies the prior art believed to be the most pertinent and, generally, rejects some or all of the patent claims as being unpatentable. (If none of the claims were rejected, this may be an indication that you did not claim all to which you were entitled.) A written response to this office action, called either a *Response* or an *Amendment,* addressing all of the issues raised by the patent examiner, must be prepared and filed—a task for which the practitioner bills by the hour. Additionally, the practitioner may interview the examiner, either by telephone or in person. In response to all of this, the examiner will, in several months, generally issue a second office action. At this point, the practitioner can usually advise whether: (1) it is highly unlikely that any worthwhile patent protection will be obtained; (2) a patent will likely issue in due course; or (3) the examiner "doesn't understand," "is unreasonable," or "is being stubborn," necessitating an appeal or other lengthy and expensive procedures. Possibilities (1) and (2) make for an easy decision. Dealing with possibility (3) is one of those situations in which decision makers earn their pay.

Once a patent issues, the Patent Office file, known as the file wrapper, is laid open to the public. Patent attorneys avidly study file wrappers as an aid to understanding the meaning of various terms and the scope of the patent claims (not surprisingly, such study is time-consuming and, hence, costly).

## Patent Marking—Little Things Mean a Lot

Before damages may be collected from a patent infringer, the patentee must establish that the infringer was warned or notified of the infringement. Once notified, damages accrue from the date of the notice. Notice may be either actual or constructive. Traditionally, *actual notice* was about what it would seem—a letter from the patentee, identifying both the patent and the infringing products and including a clear statement that the patent covered the products, or, equivalently, that the products infringed the patent. *Constructive notice,* with respect to a commercialized patent, comprises marking the patented product (or, if impractical,

**TIPS & TECHNIQUES**

Marking products with patent numbers is essential for collecting infringement damages and is also good PR for your company.

its packaging), with the patent number(s). For patents that are not commercialized, or where the commercialization does not yield a markable product, the marking requirement is excused.

Clearly, if the patentee is selling (either directly or through a licensee) patented products, it is advantageous that such products be marked with the patent number(s). Patent marking starts the damages clock ticking without the need for a notice letter to an infringer—a letter that may give the recipient standing to bring a declaratory judgment action (see Chapter 8).

## Understanding Patent Claims—Rules of the Road

As previously noted, it is the claims of a patent that determine its scope. An understanding of the basic tenets of claim construction is therefore exceedingly important.

Patent claims are composed of limitations—phrases that identify and describe, or limit, the various components (or steps, in the case of a

**TIPS & TECHNIQUES**

Claim limitations are the elements of the claim that determine the scope of the claim.

method or process claim) of the claimed invention. The various words and phrases that appear in the patent claims are to be interpreted or construed according to their normal or accustomed meaning. If no such accepted definition exists, that is, the patent draftsman has created or coined new words or phrases, or has used words or phrases in an unconventional manner (the patent draftsperson is his or her own lexicographer), the patent specification is used as a guide to claim interpretation. If no clear definition is provided in the patent specification, the file wrapper is examined. As a last resort (and only then), standard reference materials—extrinsic sources—are considered.

Every word in a patent claim is deemed to have meaning and significance. None may be ignored. Substantive patent law prohibits two patent claims from covering exactly the same invention. Thus, if (as often happens) two patent claims are largely identical, the nonidentical portions *must* be so construed as to have different meanings (this is known as the *doctrine of claim differentiation*).

Claim terms may not be construed in a manner inconsistent with arguments or statements made by the applicant during prosecution of the patent application, nor contrary to reasons that may have been enunciated by the patent examiner as the basis for claim allowance (the *doctrine of file wrapper estoppel*). (This may seem comprehensible, but wait, there's more! See Chapter 8 for remarks concerning the *Festo* case.)

Claims—actually constituent claim limitations—must be construed so as to preserve patentability. In the event that a pertinent new (not considered during the prosecution of the patent application) prior art reference is discovered, the patent claims must be interpreted, if at all possible, so as to distinguish over the reference and, hence, to maintain the validity of the claims. Also, if at all possible, claims should be construed so as to cover the embodiment(s) of the invention described in the patent specification.

If these rules seem complex and confusing, they are! As evidenced by the number of reversals handed down by the CAFC (the Court of

Appeals for the Federal Circuit—the patent appeals court), many trial judges of the federal district courts get it wrong themselves.

## Independent Claims, Dependent Claims—A Way to Simplify the Task of Claim Construction

Patent claims are of two kinds: independent claims and dependent claims. *Independent claims* are those that do not refer to another, preceding claim. Hence, the first claim of a patent (claim 1) is always independent (there *are* no preceding claims). *Dependent claims* incorporate by reference each and every limitation of each of the claims from which they depend (i.e., to which they refer). Many patents include long chains or series of dependent claims, each referring to—and incorporating the limitations of—a preceding claim. Each dependent claim is narrower (i.e., more limited in scope) than the claim from which it depends (see Chapter 8 for a more detailed explanation of this effect). Thus, if an independent claim is not infringed, no claim that depends from it (and therefore is of more limited scope) can be infringed. For this reason, attention is inevitably focused on the independent claims, which are generally much fewer in number. In most instances, the dependent claims may be safely ignored.

## Provisional Patent Rights—Life before Birth

Among the many popular misconceptions concerning patents, one of the most enduring is that patents have effect as of the date of filing. A surprising number of people believed (and continue to believe) that a patent springs to life, fully formed, upon filing. Such people occasionally wander into attorneys' offices, clutching a copy of a newly filed patent application—more often than not, an application they filed themselves—to seek enforcement of their patent against one or more alleged infringers. Such enforcement is impossible, however, because patents have effect only from the date of issue. Moreover, until recently, patents had no retroactive effect. No liability for patent infringement could arise from any activities occurring prior to the date of patent issue. However, to an extent—and *only* to an extent—this nonretroactivity of patent protection has been altered by recent changes in the patent law, which have created provisional patent rights. These same changes have also reversed the prior rule that pending patent applications be maintained in secret, by the Patent Office, until the patent issued.

Under the new law, patent applications filed on or after November 29, 2000, are published 18 months after their filing date (actually, 18 months after the earliest claimed filing date—discuss this with a patent practitioner). When an application is published, the entire file wrapper is open to inspection and copying by the public. Moreover, members of the public may, within two months of publication, submit prior art documents to the Patent Office to be considered by the patent examiner during examination of the application.

Once a patent application has been published, and an accused infringer has been given actual notice thereof, certain provisional rights apply. If the published patent application ultimately matures into an issued patent, having claims substantially similar (although as yet undecided by the courts, the term *substantially similar* probably means "virtually identical") to those previously published, the patentee—upon issue of the patent—may recover, in addition to other damages, a reasonable royalty in respect of infringement of those claims which occurred during the period between the publication of the application and the issue of the patent. Thus, a certain measure of retroactivity has been introduced into the patent system.

## Trademarks

A trademark is a word, symbol, or combination thereof that is used to identify the source, albeit a possibly anonymous source, of goods. Examples of trademarks include Nike, Rolls Royce, and Kleenex. A service mark performs the same function as a trademark with respect to the provision of services. Examples of service marks include FedEx and Roto-Rooter. A trademark or service mark has a potentially perpetual life. Although registration confers several advantages on the owner of the mark, it is not legally required. Registration may be at either the federal or state level. Marks that are unregistered are known as *common law marks*.

## Choosing a Mark

When choosing a mark, it is important to remember the function it is intended to perform, namely source identification. It is not the function of a trademark or service mark to describe the goods or services. Marketing and sales personnel frequently seek to adopt marks that describe the product or tell the customer all about it. Such efforts should be strenuously resisted. Product description should be achieved through advertising copy. Trademarks and service marks should be chosen for their distinctiveness.

Marks are categorized according to their inherent distinctiveness. The most distinctive and, hence, the most desirable marks are coined or arbitrary marks. These are either made-up words, such as Kodak or Xerox, or words that have no relation to the goods or services with which they are used, such as Camel as a trademark for cigarettes.

Next, in decreasing order of distinctiveness, are suggestive marks. These are marks that bear some relation to the goods or services with

**TIPS & TECHNIQUES**

Brands are marketing concepts and should not be confused with trademarks.

**TIPS & TECHNIQUES**

The "trade dress" of a product is comprised of the distinctive appearance of the product and/or its packaging, and may include the shape, color, and texture.

which they are used. The relation is sufficiently tenuous, however, that the goods or services are not described, nor can they be identified from knowledge of the mark alone (for example, Polar as a trademark for ice cream).

The next lower rung on the distinctiveness ladder (a significant step downward, as we shall soon see) is occupied by descriptive marks. These literally describe some feature or attribute of the goods or services, or are laudatory thereof (for example, Speedy as a service mark for a delivery service).

The bottom rung of the ladder is occupied by what are, technically, not marks at all—generic terms. A generic term is the word or phrase by which a product or service is popularly known (for example, *bicycle* is the generic term for a two-wheeled, pedal-powered vehicle). Generic terms are not protectable.

## Trademark Clearance

Trademark clearance is the process of determining or seeking to determine whether a particular mark is available for adoption and use as proposed. Just as many inventors will assure you that no patentability search is necessary because they "know the field of technology and there has never been anything like this," so too will many marketing and sales personnel assure you that no trademark clearance is necessary because they "know the market and no one is using this mark." *Do not listen to such people.* Trademark clearance (if the mark is to be used only in this country) is a relatively quick and inexpensive procedure, especially when compared with the disruptions and costs associated with unwittingly infringing the rights of another—litigation costs, damages, and the costs and chaos of suddenly changing to a new mark. If the mark is to be used abroad, it should be searched in each country where it will appear. Such searches can become costly and time consuming; therefore, plans should be made accordingly.

## Registering a Mark

While requirements and procedures vary somewhat from state to state, obtaining a state registration of a mark is most often a matter of literally filling in the blank spaces in an application form and paying a small fee. Preparing an application for federal registration is only slightly more complex. (See Appendix A for a copy of a downloadable federal trademark application form.) As a result, most (if not all) trademark attorneys prepare and file registration applications on a fixed fee basis. Formerly, use of a mark in interstate commerce was a prerequisite to filing for federal registration. In the last several years, however, the trademark law has changed, and an application for federal registration may be filed based on an intent to use the mark in interstate commerce. Nevertheless, such use must actually commence before the registration is allowed to issue.

**TIPS & TECHNIQUES**

A trade name, which is the name by which a business is known, cannot be registered as a trademark, but is governed by state and common law.

In order to perform its function—identifying the source of goods—a trademark must be distinctive. A mark that is confusingly similar to other marks cannot serve to distinguish the goods on which it is used from those of others. Some marks—coined, arbitrary, or merely suggestive marks—are deemed to be inherently distinctive. These marks are registerable *ab initio*—immediately upon adaptation and use (the reader is advised that the occasional use of Latin phrases will often impress others). Marks that lack inherent distinctiveness—descriptive marks—are registerable only upon a showing that they have achieved secondary meaning, that is, that they have become so associated with the goods, in the mind of the public, that they do, in fact, distinguish those goods. Such a showing may be made through the use of consumer surveys (very expensive) or by establishing that the applicant has used the mark continuously, and substantially exclusively, for at least five years (a so-called Section 2[f] application). This latter approach, quite obviously, requires the trademark owner to endure a lengthy (five-year) period of uncertainty before (hopefully) achieving registration of the mark. The moral of the story: avoid descriptive marks.

(*Authors' note:* The foregoing paragraph pertains primarily to the issues involved in federal registration. Some states, apparently, will register anything.)

 **TIPS & TECHNIQUES**

A trademark may be a slogan, such as Citibank's "Citi never sleeps"; or a package shape, such as the "wasp-waisted" Coca-Cola bottle; or a color, such as Dow Corning's pink fiberglass insulation.

## Valuable Trademarks

According to *Business Week*, the four most valuable trademarks in the world are Coca-Cola, Microsoft, IBM, and GE.

Like the Patent Office, the Trademark Office issues written reports in respect of applications, to which written response must be made. Here the similarity ends. In most cases, prosecution of a trademark application is much less complex and much less costly than prosecution of a patent application.

Once an application has been approved by the examining attorney, it is published for opposition—the mark, the goods or services, and the identity of the applicant are published in the weekly *Official Patent and Trademark Gazette*—and interested parties are afforded 30 days (extensions of time are freely granted) in which to file an opposition setting forth reasons why registration should be denied. If no opposition is filed, a registration issues. If an opposition is filed, there is an *inter partes proceeding* (litigation) before the Trademark Trial and Appeal Board, which decides the matter (subject, of course, to appeal).

## Proper Trademark Usage—Use It Right or Lose It

If a trademark ceases to serve primarily as an identification of the source of goods and instead comes to identify the goods themselves (i.e., if it becomes the generic term for such goods), the rights to exclusive use of the mark are lost. Notable examples of such lost marks are escalator, thermos, and aspirin. Proper trademark usage is directed to the prevention of such loss. Prior to release, all publications should be reviewed for proper trademark use. (Although the rules of proper trademark usage are beyond the scope of this book, remember: A trademark is an adjective, and should be followed by the appropriate generic term.)

It is also prudent to monitor the *Official Gazette,* so as to be able to oppose registration of marks that may cause confusion with respect to your own or may dilute or reduce the distinctiveness of your marks.

Once a mark is federally registered, it is identified by the symbol ®. The letters TM or, occasionally, SM (for service mark), are used to identify unregistered, or common-law, marks. Thus, the presence of the designation TM or SM after a mark merely means that someone is claiming proprietary rights thereto, not that the claimant actually *has* such rights. This is not meant, however, to suggest that rights claimed under common law may be safely ignored. Many unregistered marks are extremely strong. Check before proceeding.

Having now touched upon the problem of genericness, we should backtrack to an issue relating to the selection of a mark. A trademark, or service mark, is an adjective and should be used in conjunction with the appropriate generic term. If a product or service is truly the first of its kind, no accepted generic term will exist. In such case, or if the existing generic term is awkward and unwieldy—"acetylsalicylic acid" (aspirin) does not fall trippingly from the tongue—a mark may be adopted by the public as the generic term, resulting in loss of the owner's proprietary rights. To avoid such a loss, create a generic term, in addition to the trademark, and foster its adoption and use by the public; for example, "Aspirin™ pain reliever."

# Copyrights

A copyright is an exclusionary right. It conveys to its owner the right to prevent others from copying, selling, performing, displaying, or making derivative versions of a work of authorship. The duration of a copyright depends on several factors, but in no event is less than 70 years. (If your planning horizon exceeds 70 years, consult a copyright specialist.) Although registration confers several advantages on the owner of the copyright and is a prerequisite to a suit for copyright infringement, it is not legally required. Prompt registration provides remedies that make lawsuits affordable. Statutory damages of $150,000 (or more, and attorney fees) for willful infringement can be obtained if published works are registered within three months of publication or if unpublished works are registered before they are infringed.

Copyrights differ from patents in that they only protect against actual copying. A work created by another, without copying, is not an infringement, no matter how similar it may be to a copyrighted work. Moreover, copyright protects only the expression of an idea, not the idea being expressed. Thus, information or data included in a copyrighted work is not protected against appropriation and use by others, although copying of the presentation and arrangement is barred.

Copyrights are generally associated in the common mind with novels, movie scripts, music, and song lyrics. For this reason, and because of their limited scope of protection, they are often overlooked or ignored by businesspeople. Copyrights do, however, have application in the protection of product manuals and instruction booklets, training materials, and marketing and sales publications. More importantly, copyright has been utilized to protect computer software, although in recent years, computer software has often become the subject of patent applications.

## TIPS & TECHNIQUES

A copyright protects the expression of an idea, not the idea itself.

## Copyright Registration

Copyright arises automatically when the original work of authorship is affixed in a tangible medium, for example, music is written as notes on a sheet of paper, or its performance is recorded on a tape or CD. Registration of a copyright, which may be done at any time during its life, is merely a matter of filling in the blank spaces on a simple two-page form (instructions are printed on the form—see Appendix B for a sample application form), attaching (depositing) one or two copies of the subject work of authorship (see instructions) including a small (currently $30.00) filing fee, and sending it to the Library of Congress. Copyright law has no equivalent of the enablement requirement found in patent law. It is perfectly acceptable (and commonly done) to register a copyright in a computer program with significant portions of the program omitted from the copy or copies deposited. This allows registration of the copyright in the program without providing a complete and working copy to a prospective infringer.

## Copyright Notice

A copyright notice consists of the symbol ©, or the word *copyright,* followed by the year of first publication and the name of the copyright owner. Formerly, publication of a work without a copyright notice caused loss of copyright. For this reason, some people believe that they are free to copy any work that does not bear a copyright notice. *Do not listen to such people.* This aspect of the copyright law was changed more than a decade ago. While a copyright notice remains a requirement if damages are to be recovered from an infringer, the owner of a work published without a notice may obtain an injunction barring further infringement. Thus, the mere absence of a copyright notice does not indicate that a work may be freely copied. Similarly, a copyright notice should be placed on all of one's own works before they are published. To clarify a point, copyright registration is not a prerequisite to the use of a copyright notice. Thus, one may include a copyright notice in a publication before registering the copyright with the Copyright Office.

## Work for Hire—Sounds Simple, But It Isn't

A *work for hire* is, generally speaking, a work created by an employee within the scope of his or her employment, or, if the parties expressly agree in writing, a work specially commissioned for use as a contribution to a collective work.

The copyright in a work initially vests in the author or authors who created the work. However, in the case of a work for hire, the *employer* is legally considered to be the author. Thus, the copyright of such a work vests in the employer. But what about a work created by a consultant? A consultant is not an employee (if you don't believe this, just ask the IRS); and, as a result, the copyright in a work (other than a contribution to a collective work) created by a consultant will vest in the consultant, not in the client. Thus, for example, in the absence of a written copyright assignment, a computer program written by a consultant may be used by the client, but not duplicated or upgraded by the client (the upgraded program would be a *derivative work*). It is therefore extremely important to ascertain the correct employment status of all of those individuals called upon to create computer programs, advertising and promotional materials, and so on. If they are not employees, working within the scope of their employment, get a written copyright assignment.

## Fair Use—Or Foul

Not all unauthorized uses of copyrighted material constitute an infringement. Some use of others' works is permitted, even without the approval of the copyright owner. This use, known as *fair use,* is one of the most important, and least well-defined, limits to copyright protection.

**IN THE REAL WORLD**

# Copyright Infringement in the Workplace

Unlike accidents, which mostly occur in the home, copyright infringement most commonly occurs in the workplace. Otherwise honest and law-abiding citizens routinely make copies of magazine and technical journal articles and duplicate computer software, both for themselves and for their colleagues, without seeking permission from the copyright holders. If you are a part of this mob of scofflaws, beware! There are organizations hunting you.

The Copyright Clearance Center, Inc., enforces the copyrights in a vast array of periodical publications. The Clearance Center offers licenses for the copying of their clients' works and takes action against those who copy without such licenses. Similarly, the Business Software Alliance (BSA) takes action against those who make unauthorized copies of their clients' proprietary computer software. For example, in January 2001, a Chicago firm called ThoughtWorks, Inc., agreed to pay $480,000 to the BSA to settle claims of illegal use of Microsoft and IBM office productivity software by ThoughtWorks' employees.

If you are making photocopies and just can't break the habit, or have lots of unlicensed copies of software in use, it's probably best to find these folks before they find you.

The statutory basis for this doctrine, 17 United States Code §107, sets forth the factors that are to be considered in determining whether a particular use is fair use. In general, uses that advance public interests, such as criticism, comment, news reporting, teaching (including multiple copies for classroom use), scholarship, or research, are favored, while commercial uses are disfavored.

Not all commercial uses are forbidden. Most magazines and newspapers are operated for profit, yet they are not automatically precluded from availing themselves of the benefit of the doctrine. One of the most critical considerations is the "amount and substantiality of the portion used in relation to the copyrighted work as a whole." If the use is of such an extent and nature as to significantly impinge on the value of the work, or the copyright owner's income derived therefrom, it is not likely to be considered a fair use.

## Summary

A patent is the legal right to prevent others from practicing the patented invention. A patent does *not* guarantee the right of the patentee to practice the patented invention.

There are three types of patents: utility patents, design patents, and plant patents. A utility patent may cover a device or an article, a composition of matter, a method or a process of doing or making something, a new application for an existing device or material, or a product (not otherwise patentable) made by a particular new process. Design patents cover the ornamental design of an article. Plant patents cover asexually produced plants.

In order to be patentable, an invention must be novel, nonobvious, and useful. The requirement of nonobviousness is typically the most significant hurdle to be surmounted. If an invention would be obvious to one of ordinary skill in the art seeking to solve the problem addressed by the inventor, that invention is not patentable. In this regard, it is important to note that inventors and their attorneys are under an obligation to disclose to the Patent Office any prior art of which they are aware that would be relevant to the questions of novelty and nonobviousness of their invention.

Utility patents include a specification and patent claims. The specification comprises drawings and a written description of the preferred embodiment of the invention. The claims determine the scope of the patent monopoly. The specification must provide sufficient information to enable one of ordinary skill in the art to practice the patented invention (the enablement requirement).

Choice of a patent attorney is a complex question involving a trade-off between technical and legal skills. Effective cooperation with a patent attorney may minimize the cost of patent prosecution.

A trademark serves to identify the source of the goods on which it appears. A service mark serves the same function with respect to services. Marks may be registered at either the state or federal level, or they may be used without registration; such unregistered marks are known as common-law marks. Based on their level of distinctiveness, marks may be categorized as arbitrary or coined, suggestive, or descriptive.

Before adopting a mark, a search should be performed to ascertain whether it is indeed available. Once adopted, a mark should be used properly to avoid loss of exclusive rights therein.

A copyright is the right to prevent others from unauthorized reproduction, dissemination, or modification of a work of authorship. Unlike patents, copyrights do not protect against independent recreation. Although traditionally considered with respect to music, literature, and works of art, copyright now finds broad application with respect to the protection of computer software.

The exclusive rights afforded by a copyright are limited by the Doctrine of Fair Use, which allows the unauthorized copying of limited portions of another's work under certain specified circumstances.

# CHAPTER 2

# The Supporting Players: Other Types of IP

## After reading this chapter you will be able to:

- Understand the nature of trade secrets and know-how
- Understand the interplay between trade secrets and know-how and other forms of intellectual property
- Devise programs to protect trade secrets and know-how
- Understand the nature of mask works and their relationship to utility patents
- Understand the nature of registered designs and their relationship to design patents
- Register mask works and designs
- Understand and prepare noncompetition agreements and nondisclosure agreements

## Trade Secrets and Know-How

A trade secret is information that is not generally available and that confers a competitive advantage on its possessor. It may, for example, comprise a chemical formula, a manufacturing process, a machine design, or a business method. Note that the secret need not be absolute; it is necessary only that the information in question is not widely known. However, general knowledge cannot be converted into a trade secret simply by labeling it as such.

## It's Serious

Under the Economic Espionage Act of 1996, the theft of trade secrets is a federal crime, which is punishable by jail terms of up to 10 years and substantial fines.

Know-how is similar to trade secrets. Essentially, it comprises a body of information, the components of which may be individually known, but the compilation of which has competitive value. Supplier lists, parts specifications, and quality assurance and testing procedures generally fall into this category.

Unlike patents, trade secrets involve no fees or costs, and no attorneys need be retained. There are no statutory requirements and there is no uncertainty as to what, if any, protection will be secured. All that is necessary is that the subject information be treated as a secret. This is, nevertheless, a requirement that is often overlooked. Simply stated, if information is to be accorded trade secret status, it must be treated as a secret by its possessor. At a minimum, it must be marked *confidential,* and reasonable (that word again) steps should be taken to assure its security. Storage in locked cabinets, to which access is limited to those with a need to know, is generally considered a requirement, as are written confidentiality and nondisclosure agreements, executed by all those having access to the information, expressly barring any unauthorized disclosure. At the other extreme, it has been held by courts that observation of the arrangement of a partially completed chemical processing plant, from an airplane circling overhead, was improper and that reasonable steps to maintain the secret details of the plant did not necessitate erecting a roof over the whole facility.

Trade secrets are potentially immortal. Their life extends as long as the secret can be maintained. Of course, this also means that they may be extinguished, at any moment, if the information is disclosed or otherwise becomes available. Disclosure may result from inadvertence ("loose lips sink ships") or improper conduct (ranging from breaches of confidentiality obligations through industrial espionage). Moreover, the information may be independently discovered or created—actually rediscovered or recreated—by another, either by pure happenstance or through analysis or reverse engineering of the products of the trade secret owner. Herein lies an important difference between patents and trade secrets: An infringer who has independently rediscovered the patented invention is an infringer nonetheless, but not so with trade secrets. So long as the secret was rediscovered lawfully through independent research or reverse engineering, once the secret is known, it is no longer a secret and, therefore, the trade secret protection is lost. Wait, it gets worse. A competitor who has independently discovered the trade secret may patent the invention (if it is patentable) and, if successful in obtaining a patent, may actually be able to prevent the original owner from using his own trade secret.

Because they involve neither formalities nor costs, some promote trade secrets as a panacea—the preferred method of protecting virtually all intellectual property. *Do not listen to such people.* While trade secrets have their place in the panoply of intellectual property tools, they also have their limitations. They are, in fact, particularly ill suited to certain applications. Any information that can be ascertained through product examination will remain a trade secret only for so long as it takes a competitor to purchase a sample and inspect it or carry it to an analytical laboratory. As a practical matter, trade secrets are best employed as protection for manufacturing or other processing techniques that are performed in the privacy of one's own facility and that cannot be readily—if at all—discerned from an examination of the product produced thereby. A second suitable application involves information as to which only temporary protection is required. Most commonly, this involves a new product or process for which protection is sought only until market introduction—to obtain the first mover advantage. Most business methods, if not patented, should be treated as trade secrets.

Another shortcoming of trade secret protection is that, as compared to patent or copyright protection, enforcement opportunities are much more limited, and the likelihood of recovering significant damages for a violation of rights is substantially lower. Violation of trade secret rights arises only from improperly securing access to the secret information. Thus, if disclosure occurs through error—for example, if researchers talk too much at a scientific symposium (or at the bar)—no damages may be recovered from those who innocently acquire and utilize the information. Moreover, when improper activity does occur (the industrial espionage previously mentioned), damages may only be sought from the malefactor. Often, this leads only to a hollow victory.

Let us assume, for example, that a low-down, underhanded competitor bribes a technician to reveal a secret process for heat treating of machine parts to extend the useful life of certain machine tools. Assume further that this misbegotten slug then utilizes this information to produce hundreds of tools, selling them at bargain prices to one's loyalty-impaired customers. The trade secret owner promptly sues this blight on the face of the tool-producing industry, only to find, to his chagrin, that in addition to being dishonest, the odious wretch is also a poor businessperson who declares bankruptcy, leaving a hard-won (costly) judgment unsatisfied. The former customers, meanwhile, having purchased the tools without knowledge of the dastardly bribe, are free to use the same without any obligation to the trade secret's original owner. If, however, the heat treatment process had been patented (specifically, the patent would include "product by process claims" directed to tools made by this process), an entirely different result would be obtained. In this event, the patentee could sue the purchasers of the tools for *using* the tools and recover damages (hopefully in the form of lost profits—see Chapter 8).

Notwithstanding the limitations of trade secrets described here, they represent highly valuable corporate assets and are not to be treated lightly. They may afford a long-lasting monopoly and, at the very least, secure the first mover advantage. One of the most blatant misuses of trade secrets results from thoughtless mass patenting directed primarily to outnumbering the competitors in patent filings, which is practiced by some of the largest corporations. One needs to keep in mind that in obtaining a patent, one surrenders the underlying trade secret. In many instances, the exchange of a trade secret for a patent is a fair bargain. However, when patents are allowed to collect dust in corporate patent portfolios and are neither licensed nor enforced, the forfeiture of the trade secrets—the price paid for these patents—is nothing short of a total waste.

## Mask Works

Semiconductor chips, the heart and soul of the electronics age, are produced by a chemical etching process that utilizes a stencil known as a *mask work*. These chips, which may be very costly to develop, are surprisingly inexpensive to fabricate. The situation positively cries out for copying (known as *piracy* to chip developers and *free enterprise* to chip copiers).

Being useful products, semiconductor chips are not protectable by copyright (although the design drawings of the chips could be so protected—see Chapter 1). Being functional, mask works cannot be protected by design patents either. Although often complex, the chips frequently lack the nonobviousness required of a utility patent. Moreover, the current pace of technological advancement is such that chips are often obsolete within two years—less than the average period of time to process a patent application in the Patent Office.

To provide intellectual property protection under these trying conditions, Congress passed, in 1984, the Semiconductor Chip Protection Act, creating "a new form of intellectual property" (actually one closely related to a copyright, with a few patent-like aspects). The act prohibits copying of original mask works that have some degree of originality— they cannot be mere commonplace variations of previous designs (this is one of the aspects borrowed from patent law).

Registration is very similar to copyright registration and is, in fact, administered by the Copyright Office. Protection is effective upon registration or commercial exploitation (first sale, offer for sale, or other distribution to the public), whichever occurs first. However, such protection terminates two years after exploitation has begun, unless an application for protection has been filed. If registered, protection runs for 10 years from the time it began.

Although it is not required, the owner of a mask work may affix a notice (comprising the words "mask work," the symbol **M** or the letter *M* in a circle, and the name or designation of the owner) on packaging for products employing the mask work, thereby giving constructive notice of its protected status.

# Registered Designs

Many industrial designs pose the same problems with regard to legal protection that are presented by mask works: While novel, they are not nonobvious (and, hence, not protectable by a design patent), and the designs have a commercial or market life that is short relative to the average period of time to process a design patent application in the Patent

Office. Not surprisingly, the solution to this problem—design registration—is quite similar to the solution to the comparable problem posed by mask works.

Original designs for useful articles may be registered through a process akin to the registration of a copyright or mask work. The registration must be filed within one year of the first public disclosure of the design, or protection is barred. Protection of the design commences upon the earlier of the date of registration or the date the design was first made public, and extends for a term of 10 years.

Registration is barred, however, for designs that are dictated solely by utilitarian function, that are commonplace, or that are insignificant variations of commonplace designs. Registered designs may be marked with a notice, similar to a copyright notice, including the words *Protected Design,* the abbreviation *Prot'd Des.,* the letter *D* within a circle, or the symbol **D**. The notice should also include the year in which protection for the design first commenced and the name or designation of the owner. Although marking is not mandatory, it is highly advisable, as it constitutes constructive notice of the owner's rights.

## Noncompetition Agreements and Confidential Disclosure Agreements

Employees (broadly defined) comprise a firm's human capital, a constituent ingredient of intellectual capital. Departing employees deplete a firm's stock of intellectual capital. Worse, they may convey a firm's intellectual capital to a competitor. Indeed, who would value a firm's intellectual capital more highly than its competitors? How, then, is a firm to prevent its intellectual capital from falling into the hands of its competitors? The obvious solution to this problem was barred by the ratification of the Thirteenth Amendment to the Constitution, prohibiting involuntary servitude. The next best solution is the noncompetition agreement.

A noncompetition agreement is a contractual undertaking (lawyer-speak for *agreement*) between an employee and his or her employer. The agreement limits the right of the employee, upon departure, to accept employment with a competitor of his or her former employer. Non-competition agreements create a conflict between two public policy considerations: the need of an employer to protect its intellectual capital and the need of a departing employee to secure suitable new employment. Resolution of this conflict is achieved by requiring that the scope of the agreement be limited to that which is clearly necessary to protect the employer, and no more. The limitations are of three kinds: temporal, geographic, and scope.

Temporal limitations refer to the duration of the agreement, that is, the time that must elapse before a departing employee may accept employment with a competitor. The employer's goal is to allow sufficient time for the knowledge held by the departing employee to become obsolete or stale. Obviously, from the employer's perspective, the longer the time period is, the better. However, it is wise to remember that the reasonableness of any temporal limitation is a question of fact, to be decided by a jury, and that employees are likely to outnumber

**IN THE REAL WORLD**

## Limiting an Employee's Invention Assignments

Some states, including California and Illinois, have enacted statutes that restrict the scope of Employee Invention Assignment agreements. Generally, under such statutes, employees are only obligated to assign those inventions made during the course of employment and at the employer's direction.

employers on any jury. As a practical matter, any period beyond three years is likely to be considered highly suspect.

Geographic limitations refer to the geographic area in which the departing employee may not accept employment with a competitor during the agreed-on time period. Such limitations are based on the premise that the employer's business is limited to a specific geographic market and that the departing employee's activities outside this market area cannot harm the former employer. Geographical limitations work well for purely local businesses such as beauticians and barbers, dry cleaners, carpenters, and the like; however, given the national, if not global, nature of most business today, there is a serious question as to the continued validity or relevance of this premise. If, however, the employer's business is truly regional, such a limitation may provide a workable means of resolving the conflict.

Finally, breadth (also known as scope) limitations refer to the definition of *competitor.* For example, if one is in the plumbing supply business, is "the competition" limited to other plumbing supply companies, or does it include all hardware firms? Today, many firms comprise more than one business. This is especially true in the case of vertically integrated businesses and conglomerates. The competitors of such firms are legion. (Consider, for example, how many firms compete—in one way or another—with some component of General Electric Corporation.) It is necessary therefore to define the scope of the prohibition as narrowly as possible. Remember, the goal is merely to prevent the departing employee from utilizing confidential knowledge to the former employer's detriment.

Confidential disclosure agreements, known as nondisclosure agreements (NDAs), are conceptually related to noncompetition agreements. Each is, in essence, an agreement that the recipient of specified information will use that information only for a specified purpose and will maintain it in confidence. Although public policy issues applicable to noncompetition agreements do not influence nondisclosure agreements, they are subject to certain practical considerations. Because they are so widely used, it is worthwhile to carefully explore and understand these limitations.

Before accepting information in confidence, the prospective recipient should assure herself that the obligations of confidentiality and limited use, at a minimum, will not restrict her from using information already in her possession or information that may subsequently come into her possession from another source, free of any burdens. Obviously, such assurance is difficult, if not impossible to obtain, in part because the recipient often cannot ascertain in advance exactly what information will be disclosed, and also in part because the recipient often cannot ascertain exactly what information her firm already possesses. Moreover, lacking prescience, the intended recipient has no ability to foresee what information may come into her possession in the future or may be independently developed by her staff.

Excepting certain information from the obligations imposed by the confidential disclosure agreement most commonly solves this problem. Although the precise language utilized may vary somewhat, these exceptions apply to information that is:

- In the public domain
- Already in the possession of the recipient
- Subsequently comes into the possession of the recipient, from a source not known by the recipient to be under any obligation of confidentiality
- Is disclosed by the owner of the information to a third party without any obligation of confidentiality
- Is subsequently independently created by the recipient without recourse to the disclosed materials (This last exception is often the subject of some disagreement, as it requires a high degree of trust.)

Notwithstanding the presence of these standard exceptions, the intended recipient should seek as clear—and narrow—as possible a description of the information to be disclosed. Finally, there should be a time limit on the obligation. Ideally, it should expire when the information to be conveyed has become stale. Commonly, confidential disclosure agreements have terms not exceeding three years. See Appendix C for a sample Nondisclosure Agreement.

## Summary

Trade secrets are information not generally known that confers a competitive advantage upon its possessor. Similarly, know-how is a body of information, the components of which may be individually known, but the compilation of which has competitive value. Reasonable steps must be taken to preserve the confidentiality of trade secrets and know-how.

Trade secrets and know-how may be lost through inadvertence, improper activity (industrial espionage), or through independent recreation, including recreation resulting from reverse engineering. When improper activity does occur, only the actual wrongdoer is liable for damages.

Trade secrets are forfeited when disclosed in a patent application. The surrender of the trade secret is the price one pays for obtaining a patent.

Both mask works, which are the stencils used in the fabrication of semiconductor chips, and designs of useful articles, may be legally protected by registration in the Copyright Office. Such registrations provide quick and inexpensive, albeit limited, intellectual property protection.

Noncompetition agreements limit the right of a departing employee to accept employment with a competitor of his or her former employer. These agreements are designed to protect the intellectual capital of the employer, and public policy dictates that such agreements include such temporal, geographic, and breadth limitations as to not unduly bar the former employee from securing new employment.

Confidential disclosure agreements, also known as NDAs, are intended to allow a controlled, or limited, disclosure of confidential information. Under such an agreement, the recipient of proprietary information agrees to maintain it in confidence and to use it only for specified purposes.

Exhibits 2.1 and 2.2 provide a quick reference on the various types of IP, their terms, and a sampling of the types of intellectual assets that they may be used to protect. These exhibits are for illustration purposes only. Many exceptions exist, and in every instance, a professional should be consulted. The applicability of any IP tool is dependent on the particular facts of the situation.

**EXHIBIT 2.1**

# Comparative Table of Intellectual Properties

| | Utility Patent | Design Patent | Trademark/ Service mark | Copyright | Trade Secret | Mask Work | Registered Design |
|---|---|---|---|---|---|---|---|
| **Protects** | Products, devices, processes, business methods | Industrial design | Words, phrases, or symbols that identify the source of goods or service | Expressions of creative works, such as pictures, novels, music performance, advertising copy, etc. | Confidential information that is maintained secret | Mask works – stencils used for semiconductor chip manufacturing | Industrial designs |
| **Term (in years)** | 20 | 14 | Perpetual, so long as used | 70 minimum | Perpetual, as long as secret is maintained | 10 | 10 |
| **Registration required** | Yes | Yes | No | No | No | Yes | Yes |
| **Examined** | Yes | Yes | Yes | No | N/A | No | No |
| **Cost to Obtain and Maintain** | High | Medium | Low | Low | Low | Low | Low |

**EXHIBIT 2.2**

# Intellectual Property Protection Table

| | Utility Patent | Design Patent | Trademark/ Service mark | Copyright | Trade Secret | Mask Work | Registered Design |
|---|---|---|---|---|---|---|---|
| Article of Manufacture | Yes | Yes | | | Possibly | | Yes |
| Manufacturing Process | Yes | | | | Possibly | | |
| Computer Software | Yes | | | Yes | Possibly | | |
| Business Method | Yes | | | | Possibly | | |
| Brand Name | | | Yes | | | | |
| Product Manual | | | | Yes | | | |
| Training Manual | | | | Yes | Yes | | |
| Semiconductor Chip | | | | | | Yes | |
| Corporate Logo | | | Yes | | | | |
| Chemical Compound | Yes | | | | Possibly | | |
| Fabric Print Pattern | | Yes | | | | | Yes |
| Photograph | | | | Yes | | | |
| Novel | | | | Yes | | | |
| Movie Script | | | | Yes | | | |
| Musical Performance | | | | Yes | | | |
| Series of Movements in Sports | Yes | | | | | | |
| Web Page | | Yes | | Yes | | | Yes |
| Internet Domain | | | Possibly | | | | |

# CHAPTER 3

# Protecting the Fruits of Your R&D

## After reading this chapter you will be able to:

- Recognize the importance of proper disclosure in protecting an invention
- Successfully motivate inventors
- Understand the parts of the invention disclosure form
- Ensure that anything invented by your employees for your company actually *belongs* to your company

## Getting It Down on Paper

Developing new technology is only half the battle. The technology or any other intellectual asset must be protected if its potential value is to be fully realized.

**TIPS & TECHNIQUES**

Laboratory notebooks are necessary for every R&D project. Each step of the inventive process should be carefully documented in a lab notebook on a daily basis and every page must be dated and witnessed by two people, other than the inventor(s).

Intellectual capital is a creation of the mind. Before it can be protected or even used, it must be disclosed by its creators(s). More specifically, it must be disclosed to those who will be responsible for its use and those who will undertake to secure and protect it.

Proper disclosure is particularly important with respect to inventions that may be susceptible of protection by patenting or as trade secrets. Obviously, no steps can be taken to protect an invention until its existence and nature are known. Unless suitably encouraged and directed, many inventors will not disclose their inventions in such manner as to bring them to the prompt attention of those charged with securing and protecting them. Some inventors are too busy with other tasks, or simply too lazy, to prepare a proper disclosure of their work. Some inventors are excessively humble, refusing to recognize the significance (and value) of their work. Some do not understand intellectual property and the rules pertaining to its protection. Such lack of understanding can be overcome by periodic, brief talks or presentations.

Organizations are well advised to prepare standardized invention disclosure forms and to include invention disclosure and a performance review into research and development (R&D) staff job descriptions, as well as those of middle management (remember, business methods and processes can now also be patented).

The other hindrances to disclosure are best overcome by resorting to that most powerful of human motivators—self-interest (there's no interest like self-interest).

Many organizations, especially larger organizations with long and depersonalizing channels of communications, institute what are known as *inventor award* or *inventor incentive* programs. Although these programs vary in detail, they generally provide a cash reward to the inventor or co-inventors when a patent application is filed. A second, generally larger, reward is paid to the inventor(s) upon the issue of a patent. The purpose of this second reward is to induce the inventor(s) to cooperate in the prosecution of the patent application. In many instances, these rewards are inadequate and fail to sufficiently motivate personnel.

It should be noted that these rewards are not in the nature of compensation for the invention. Rather, they are a token—a form of acknowledgment or recognition of the contribution the inventor has made to the firm. Attempts to compensate inventors with a portion of the profits earned from their inventions have proven counterproductive. Although not common in this country, such programs are mandated by law in several European countries. To the extent that they were intended to encourage innovation, such programs have failed. The major results seem to be suspicion, on the part of inventors, that they are being cheated (management, after all, does the bookkeeping), anger on the part of those not named as co-inventors, corporate politicking to have one's invention commercialized, jealousy, and, in general, a balkanization of the workforce. Moreover, the ability to license or assign IP rights is compromised by the demands of the inventors who, in effect, become parties to any negotiations. It may prove more productive to reward the inventors with a one-time monetary award of appreciable value.

In virtually all organizations, the creation of inventions is subject to the Parado 80/20 Rule: 80% of the inventions are created by 20% of the technical staff (note that the term *engineers* was not used—many of the most prolific inventors are mere designers). Identify these people and keep them happy.

## The Invention Disclosure Form

Invention disclosure forms are adapted to elicit from the inventor(s) the information that is required for the preparation of a patent application. A sample disclosure form may be found in Appendix E. As seen in the illustration, such forms typically request a brief description of the problem

**TIPS & TECHNIQUES**

To establish the conception date of an invention one may utilize such Internet-based "digital notary" services as *www.firstuse.com, www. e-timestamp.com, www.digistamp.com,* and *www.surety.com.*

being solved by the invention and a description of the prior solutions, or attempted solutions, and the reasons why they were not wholly satisfactory. Identification of known prior art is requested. A description of the invention is also requested, preferably to include drawings or sketches. Next, the inventor(s) is generally requested to highlight those aspects of the invention believed to be novel and to consider what modifications or alterations could be made to the invention. These questions are intended to elicit information of use in the preparation of the patent claims. Finally, questions are often presented as to possible applications of the invention, date of first sale, offer for sale, or disclosure of the invention in a written publication, its estimated value or significance, and where it is likely to be of use. These last questions are intended to elicit information of use in establishing priorities as to the filing of patent applications and in identifying those foreign countries where patent protection should be sought (more on this issue later).

It is also worthwhile to ask the inventor(s) to identify possible uses of the invention in the industries other than those in which the organization competes. This may facilitate the future licensing of the invention to others.

It will be recalled that patent practitioners most commonly bill by the hour for time spent in drafting patent applications. It should be appreciated therefore that a well-prepared invention disclosure will not only improve the quality of a patent application based thereon but will also reduce the cost of such an application by reducing the amount of time the patent practitioner must devote to its preparation. In an ideal situation, the patent practitioner would merely be required to draft the patent claims—in fact, such a method of preparing patent applications is widely utilized in Japan. The quality of patent disclosure becomes even more important in situations in which a patent practitioner has little or no contact with the inventor, and thus has only the invention disclosure to work with.

## Make Sure You Own It

Probably few things are as frustrating, or embarrassing, or potentially career-threatening as creating, or having created for you, a valuable piece of intellectual property, only to find that you lost it or, perhaps worse, don't own it—it is owned by someone else.

It is well settled in the law that inventions made in the course of their employment, by individuals whose duties encompass such inventive efforts, belong to the employer. Notwithstanding, it has been common practice (which one should follow) to have those employees involved in tasks likely to result in the creation of inventions, that is, engineers, product designers, and more recently, software designers, execute written agreements, known as *invention assignment agreements,* acknowledging that any invention that they may make in the course of their employment, belongs to their employer and obligating them to disclose such inventions and to cooperate in securing patent or other protection therefore. A sample invention assignment agreement is found in Appendix D.

Today, however, the advent of business method patents has opened the Patent Office doors to a host of professionals, such as accountants, salespeople, and marketing specialists, who were not formerly considered potential inventors and therefore were not traditionally required to execute invention assignment agreements. These days, *all* employees should be required to execute invention assignment agreements. (Caution—this matter should be reviewed with a labor lawyer. Ask about the need for additional consideration.)

Not all inventions are patentable. Some inventions that are patentable should (for reasons that will be discussed later) be left unpatented. Many such inventions, however, can still be protected as trade secrets if they are maintained in confidence. Thus, after disclosure (our old friend, the invention disclosure form), they must be maintained in confidence. For this reason (and others) it is important that all personnel with access to confidential information (practically everyone) give a vow of silence. Such vows, when made in a business setting, are generally known as *confidentiality agreements.* A sample confidentiality agreement is found in Appendix C.

## Plan Ahead for Protection

Many business corporations (and individual inventors) consider patents only when an invention is completed and ready to bring to market. Indeed, many prospective patentees wait until literally the last day before filing a patent application (occasionally, they wait until the day *after* the last day, creating ulcers for patent attorneys' malpractice insurance carriers). This approach, known as *retrospective patenting,* is primarily defensive in nature—it is intended to defend the market for the new product. Moreover, such corporations typically limit, or narrowly focus, their inventive efforts to what is considered core business areas and, as a result, develop correspondingly limited or narrow patent portfolios. They view patents as valuable only with regard to technology that falls within the scope of their current business.

Increasingly, however, inventions are being patented before the invention has been demonstrated physically. Instead of awaiting the building, testing, and refining of prototypes before seeking patent protection, many inventors are now filing patent applications in respect of the results of thought experiments. This approach is known as *prospective patenting.* There seems to be a strong probability that retrospective patents will be defensive or core patents, while prospective patents are rather likely to be offensive or noncore patents.

In addition to the traditional function of protecting the market for a newly developed product, prospective patents are also being used as bargaining chips for cross-licensing negotiations with other organizations, allowing a patentee to trade away patent protection for an invention it chooses not to commercialize, in exchange for the right to proceed with respect to a product otherwise blocked by a competitor's patent(s). Prospective patents, comprising bases for potential counterclaims, may also serve to discourage competitors from crossing litigation swords with the patentee. They may add revenue through licensing or sale and, in today's economy, they may facilitate (or even enable) the patentee to raise capital.

## Summary

An invention can be protected only after it has been disclosed to those responsible for its protection. The invention disclosure form is a vehicle for securing such disclosure. Various inventor award or inventor incentive programs may be organized to encourage disclosure of inventions and cooperation in securing protection for those inventions.

An organization should ensure that it will own the inventions and other intellectual assets created by its employees. This may be accomplished through use of invention assignment agreements.

# CHAPTER 4

# Know What You Have (IP Audit) and What the Other Guy Has (Competitive Intelligence)

## After reading this chapter you will be able to:

- Know the goals of an intellectual property audit
- Understand the advantages conferred by having an outside organization (rather than in-house personnel) perform the IP audit
- Identify core, noncore, and useless patents in your portfolio
- Gain useful information about your competitors' business and product plans through monitoring their patents and patent applications
- Understand patent mapping's advantages and limitations

## The Intellectual Property Audit

Often, a firm does not know or may not fully appreciate the scope and applicability of its intellectual property. To paraphrase one business executive, "Had we known then what we know now, we would be twice the size." The means to correct this lack of knowledge is an intellectual property audit.

An intellectual property audit has several goals:
- To identify all of the intellectual property a firm may possess
- To assure that all identified property is properly assigned and protected
- To identify intellectual assets that are worth protecting, thereby converting them into intellectual property
- To identify any gaps in the systematic extraction of knowledge and converting intellectual capital into intellectual assets
- To identify any gaps, problems, or failures in the procedures followed by a firm in identifying and safeguarding such assets

The audit can, theoretically, be performed by either an outside organization, such as an intellectual property law firm or intellectual property management firm, or done in-house. While the in-house approach offers a clear advantage (it's free), it is almost always the worse choice. Essentially, doing an effective audit in-house requires that the personnel involved either: (1) admit to their own shortcomings and mistakes (not likely); or (2) point out the shortcomings and mistakes of their colleagues (everyone knows where that leads). Let the professionals handle it—it's worth the cost.

Typically, at the commencement of the audit, the auditors will submit a detailed list of questions to be answered by the firm being audited (hereafter the "auditee"). Submission of this questionnaire is often followed by a meeting with liaison personnel and key executives of the auditee, where the questions are discussed and explained.

The questionnaire is largely designed to elicit information as to what intellectual property has been created or acquired, and what steps (if any) have been taken to protect this property. A thorough audit will also delve into the procedures followed by the auditee in documenting and protecting its intellectual property. A sample Intellectual Property Audit Questionnaire may be found in Appendix E.

Based on the answers to the questionnaire, and the results of follow-up investigations, an inventory of intellectual property is produced. This inventory generally includes both an identification of the individual items and a description of their legal status. Recommendations are provided as to any further steps to be taken to protect or secure these specific items. Often, an audit will indicate that intellectual assets *may* have been created in the course of a given project or program, or that there exists a substantial probability that assets may, in the future, be so created. In the former event, further analysis may be required before a definite response can be provided. In the latter event, a heightened awareness and careful monitoring of the project or program is generally prescribed.

In this regard, it should be considered that intellectual property is, potentially, being created whenever and wherever efforts are being directed to the solution of a problem or the satisfaction of a need. This concept is generally accepted with respect to technological research and product development. It also applies, however, to market research, preparation of sales and promotional materials, and development of accounting and control systems and new methods of doing business. Tools are available that, under the appropriate circumstances, may provide for the protection of the results of all of these efforts. Examine everything. Overlook or ignore nothing.

In addition to recommendations with respect to individual property items and specific projects or programs, an intellectual property audit should include policy or procedural recommendations directed to the identification and protection of intellectual property that may be created in the future. Once such policies and procedures have been adopted and implemented—and with the experience gained through participation in the audit process—subsequent, periodic audits may be adequately performed in-house. Nevertheless, independent (diplomatic way to say "outside") personnel should perform audits upon the occurrence of

## Don't Assume—Verify

Even large, supposedly sophisticated organizations screw up occasionally. Recently, the Volkswagen Group purchased all of the assets of the Rolls Royce Motor Car Company. Volkswagen acquired the plant, equipment, parts, and tooling. To their surprise and chagrin, however, Volkswagen did *not* get the famous Rolls Royce trademark. Subsequent investigation revealed that the Rolls Royce Motor Car Company did not own the trademark; rather, the Rolls Royce airplane engine company, a completely separate entity, owned it. Moreover, under its terms, the license terminated upon a change in ownership by the car company.

critical or unusual events, such as the acquisition or divestiture of a business unit, or when the business to be audited is a joint venture with another party.

Without proper invention assignment agreements, the firm may not own all of the IP discovered by the IP audit. Therefore, the audit should include a review of all consulting agreements and verification that all employees have executed invention assignment agreements and nondisclosure agreements (NDAs).

In the event of a recent merger or acquisition, the IP audit should assure that the surviving entity not only owns intellectual assets contractually, but that the transfer of ownership had been properly recorded (e.g., patent assignments were recorded in USPTO).

## The Patent Review Committee

One of the questions that must be answered with respect to each (hopefully) patentable invention is where (in which countries) patent protection is to be sought. A subsequent question, which should be raised and answered after a patent issues, is whether maintenance of the patent (i.e., payment of the periodic government patent maintenance fees) is economically justified. These questions are best answered by a patent committee.

A patent committee generally includes, at a minimum, representatives from the legal, marketing, and engineering departments. In some cases, the engineering contingent may include specialists in manufacturing, product development and basic research. Collectively, the committee members should be aware of the current state of their employer's product plans (emphasis on *current*) and the available intelligence as to the products, processes, and plans of competitors. In addition, they should possess the breadth of technical expertise and foresight to assess the present and future applicability or utility of an invention. If available, an in-house patent practitioner and a licensing executive should also be included.

It is the function of the committee to periodically review the entire patent portfolio, including invention disclosures, pending patent applications and issued patents, to decide:

- Which invention disclosures should be made the subjects of patent applications
- Whether continued prosecution of pending patent application is warranted
- Whether foreign patent protection is to be sought and, if so, in which countries
- Whether issued patents should be maintained or allowed to lapse

The appropriate frequency of meetings is proportional to the size of the portfolio to be reviewed and, to a somewhat lesser extent, to the rate of change of plans and technologies in the industry. The committee should hold meetings at least quarterly. Most large organizations hold monthly meetings.

The importance of the committee in protecting the organization's intellectual property, while still controlling costs, should be emphasized. Because committee deliberations occupy time that would otherwise be devoted to meeting departmental goals, departmental heads may be inclined to delegate their least productive personnel for committee membership (this kind of selection process should be familiar to those with military experience). A committee composed of such people may well be worse than no committee at all. Every effort should be made to assure all concerned that the committee is composed of the most—not the least—capable personnel.

In the event the IP audit is conducted internally (which is not recommended), the place to start may be to create simple schedules of all patents, trademarks, service marks, copyrighted materials, trade secrets, etc.

After the schedules have been compiled, remove expired or lapsed patents and trademarks and verify the status of every intellectual asset identified (if some of the rights have recently lapsed, such as for failure to pay patent maintenance fees, they may be reinstated if acted upon immediately).

Create a schedule of critical dates (on which patent maintenance fees must be paid or licenses renewed, etc.) and create a mechanism to act timely to prevent future loss of rights.

## Portfolio Audit—Triage for Patents

An intellectual property audit is directed to the identification and protection of intellectual property. A portfolio audit, which may be considered the next step in the IP utilization process, sorts through the patents in a portfolio in order to separate the wheat from the chaff.

Over the years, large companies tend to accumulate significant numbers of patents in their portfolios. Some of these patents are acquired as the result of corporate mergers and acquisitions. Many such patents are "orphans"—unknown and unloved by anyone at the acquiring or surviving company. Another cause of portfolio growth (or bloat) is the natural reluctance of anyone to take responsibility for abandoning a patent or pending patent application. New patents are constantly added to the portfolio, but none, or few, are deleted (rather like the Roach Motel—"they check in, but they don't check out").

The maintenance of a patent portfolio involves both direct, or explicit, costs and indirect, or implicit, costs. The direct costs are, of course, the prosecution costs and maintenance fees incurred in prosecuting, and subsequently maintaining, the patents in the portfolio. Less obviously but more importantly, the indirect cost is the loss of value of the trade secrets disclosed in the patent application. The indirect costs are also the so-called opportunity costs—the revenues foregone by failure to license patents that are of interest to others and the losses suffered as the result of failure to enforce those patents which are being infringed. To the extent that funds are being expended in prosecuting patent applications and maintaining issued patents that do not further business objectives, such expenditures are wasted.

Similarly (although less noticeably), the failure to extract value from the patent portfolio also comprises a waste of the business's assets. Effective management (and retention of cushy jobs) requires that such waste be avoided or eliminated (for more on the exciting topic of "Who's Responsible?," see Chapter 7).

The patents and patent applications that comprise the patent portfolio may be divided into three categories: core, noncore, and useless.

Core patents are those that cover key technologies. They provide exclusivity with regard to production processes, products, or services of the enterprise. Core patents are to be vigorously enforced so as to maintain the exclusive franchise they were intended to secure. Failure to enforce core patents results in the two great ills attendant upon competition—loss of market share and price erosion.

Noncore patents are those that cover technologies that are useful, or potentially useful, but not critical to a firm's competitive position. They may, for example, pertain to products or services that the firm has decided not to market or to processes it has chosen not to utilize. These very products, processes or services may, however, be of interest to others (*interest* means "willing to pay"). Thus, revenues may be realized by the assignment (lawyerspeak for "sale") or licensing of noncore patents (see the "Liability" section regarding the licensing of core patents). Such businesses, however, will rarely beat a path to your door. Licensing of noncore patents is a complex and time-consuming (although often extremely lucrative) task (see Chapter 6). Setting up a patent licensing or IP management group dedicated to extracting value from the existing IP portfolio may prove to be a very worthwhile undertaking.

Useless patents are exactly what they would seem to be. Generally, they pertain to obsolete technologies or to technologies that seemed promising but failed to develop as anticipated—technological "dead ends." In other cases, they may represent sound technological developments that were sidestepped by the standard-setting bodies, rendering them mostly useless. They confer no competitive advantage and offer no reasonable likelihood of generating any revenues. A business should cut its losses and abandon such patents.

Who is to perform this patent triage? The answer is, primarily, the Patent Review Committee. Indeed, if the Committee has been properly fulfilling its role, there should be no such accumulation of useless patents—such patents would be promptly identified and abandoned. Similarly, in making its group decision that an invention merited the filing of a patent application, the committee had determined that it was either critical to the firm's competitive position (a core patent), or held the promise of financial gain (a noncore patent). This preliminary decision was revisited each time the Committee considered further expenditures with respect to the patent application—prosecution costs, issue fees, foreign filing costs, and maintenance fees.

Occasionally, due to changes in a firm's plans, an invention once thought to be critical may be downgraded to noncore status. (Changes in the state of the art or developmental failures generally result in an invention being considered useless.) It is a function of the Committee to react to such changes. The Committee should have, in effect, if not in fact, a list of noncore patents ripe and ready for licensing. The Committee members should also be able to offer much useful advice as to potential uses and licensees of such technologies.

## Competitive Intelligence

### Patent Judo—Turning Your Competitors' Strength Against Them

In business, there are two kinds of patents: (1) one's own and (2) one's competitors'. The first kind of patents protect the fruits of an organization's skill, labor, creativity, and capital investment. They prevent unimaginative, unprincipled, and ruthless competitors, both present and potential, from misappropriating the organization's work—reaping where they did not sow, stealing the organization's inventions.

The competitors' patents are monopolistic tools—obstacles to market entry that stifle competition. One cannot be too objective about this —one's own patents are assets, one's competitors' patents are a problem. It all depends on one's vantage point.

Obviously, significant benefits flow from the first kind of patents and, for this reason, such patents are or should be a matter of serious attention. Less obviously, value can also be derived from the second kind of patents—those owned by competitors—as they contain much valuable information about such competitors' developments, products, and plans; and, for this reason, they too should be accorded a measure of attention.

Each of a competitors' patents describes a product, or a process, or an improvement in a product or process, which that competitor believes to be of sufficient value to warrant its cost (practitioner's fees, for drafting and prosecution, filing fees, issue fees, and maintenance fees, not to mention the loss of the value of the underlying trade secret forfeited in the patent application). Clearly, one should not ascribe too much significance to a single patent or published patent application. Plans and markets may change, and apparently promising developments may prove to be limited or flawed. Nevertheless, a competitor's patent, at a minimum, identifies a technology or product of interest to the patentee. Moreover, the existence of multiple patents on closely related technologies or products might be considered a reliable predictor of future activity. Simply stated, the competitor is paying a lot of money to tell the world what he plans to do, and it would be ungracious and downright foolish not to take appropriate notice.

There are several ways in which this valuable information may be obtained. The least costly method is to simply examine the *Official Patent and Trademark Gazette*. This publication contains the abstract and a representative drawing from each patent issued in the previous week, together with the name(s) of the inventor(s) and (if the patent has been assigned) the name of the assignee. The patents are arranged, in the *Gazette*, according to their Patent Office classification. Thus, all patents pertaining to a given field of technology are grouped together and may be readily scanned to identify those of interest.

In addition, the *Gazette* includes both inventor and assignee indices, permitting the ready identification of patents assigned to particular competitors or those with particular inventors. Once patents of interest have been identified, copies may be ordered from the Patent Office or obtained online from any of a variety of providers. Alternatively, a standing order may be placed with the United States Patent and Trademark Office (USPTO) for copies of all patents issuing in designated technological areas. A patent practitioner may perform the same continual monitoring of newly issued patents—not surprisingly, this is known as a *patent watch*. (Practitioners are generally eager to provide such services as they provide an opportunity to bill at substantial rates for work done by paralegals or clerks or, sometimes, computers.) Such patent watches may be limited to U.S. patents and published patent applications or may extend to European (EPO) and Japanese patent applications, which are "laid open" or published prior to issue.

Formerly, U.S. patent applications were maintained in confidence, and one would need to monitor the Patent Cooperation Treaty (PTO) filings, which are published after 18 months, in order to gain a glimpse of the content of the corresponding U.S. patent applications. However, as noted in Chapter 2, all patent applications filed in the United States after November 29, 2000, will also be published after 18 months. (Some

**TIPS & TECHNIQUES**

Most patent searches can be done now on the Internet and can easily be automated. Information providers such as Nerac, Inc. (*www.nerac.com*) can monitor all newly issued patents, identifying those that are assigned to a particular company, pertain to a particular technology, to a classification code, or that contain keyword(s) of interest.

inventors may opt to forgo filing corresponding foreign patent applications and request that their applications be kept secret in the USPTO.)

To search for U.S. patents, one may also visit the web site of the USPTO (*www.uspto.gov*), or the Delphion Intellectual Property Network (*www.delphion.com*). One of the most useful databases is the Derwent World Patents Index (*www.derwent.com*).

One can similarly monitor scientific and technical literature for any articles either published by competitors' staff, pertaining to a particular field of technology, or containing certain keywords. Such services are provided, for example, by Nerac.

Further information on a competitor's activities may be gleaned by closely examining the front pages of the competitor's patents. Patent title pages contain a wealth of information, including lists of the "prior art" cited during the prosecution of the patent. Prior art citations in a patent are of three kinds: (1) U.S. patents, (2) foreign patents, and (3) research publications (scientific papers and conference proceedings) and other nonpatented prior art. Calculating the median age of the cited patents, a parameter called Technology Cycle Time (TCT) may help in deducing how close the competitor's R&D activities are to cutting-edge research. Citation of more recent patents may indicate that the R&D program is in step with or at least close to the state of the art, while a predominance of old patent citations may indicate that the development activities are merely directed toward improvements of old technology.

Similarly, the mean number of references to scientific publications among the patents issued to a company, called the Science Linkage index, may reveal whether this company's R&D program is directed more to basic research or to product development. A predominant focus on basic research indicates long term planning that may secure such a firm a future competitive advantage (more on this in Chapter 10). Similar watch programs may (and should) be implemented with respect to a firm's trademarks and copyrighted materials.

## Signs of Opportunity

The question is often asked (or should be), "How can I find out who, if anyone, is infringing my patent?" One answer to this question is, "Look at other people's patents."

Conveniently printed on the top sheet of each patent is a list of the prior art references cited during the course of its prosecution. In a broad sense, these prior art references identify the technology on which the patented invention rests. Stated in another way, the patented invention is, to a greater or lesser degree, an improvement on the cited prior art. Remember the red fire engine. If a patent is cited as prior art in a patent owned by another inventor, then it is quite possible that practice of the other's invention will constitute an infringement of the patent cited as prior art.

Monitor newly issued patents—especially those assigned to competitors—to identify those wherein your patent is cited as prior art. If such a patent is found, determine whether the assignee of that patent is practicing the patented invention. If the patented invention *is* being practiced, carefully examine the patented product or service to determine whether infringement has occurred. There may well be a patent enforcement opportunity (patent infringement is an enforcement opportunity in the same way that a cruise on the *Titanic* was a swimming opportunity). If the newly identified patentee is not practicing its own patented invention, this may be due to a variety of factors, including concern over infringement of the cited prior art patent. Thus, this may be a licensing opportunity.

## Patent Mapping

One of the popular topics in current writings on intellectual property is patent mapping. Patent mapping sounds terribly complex, but in actuality, it is quite simple. Patent mapping, simply stated, is the visual—actually, graphical or tabular—presentation of patent data. The data being presented may relate to one's own patents, or to patents of competitors (i.e., competitive intelligence data).

Among the more common applications of patent mapping are the following:

- *Benchmarking.* This is a presentation of the number of patents held by various competitors, especially those that are considered to be the "best of breed." The numbers may be simply presented in gross (the total number of patents owned by an organization) or they may be divided into classes based on subject matter. Benchmarking is intended to facilitate the comparison of a firm's intellectual property portfolio with the corresponding portfolios of its competitors. The weakness of this analysis, however, is that it fails to account for patent quality. Rather, it rests on the implicit assumption that all patents are of equal scope, equal validity and enforceability, and, hence, of equal value, which, of course, is not so.

- *Competitive predictions.* As previously noted, an analysis of a competitor's patent portfolio can help predict new products and the overall direction the competitor is likely to take. This analysis can be refined if one focuses on the *changes* in a portfolio (i.e., what is the competitor patenting *now?*). Such current efforts can be masked if one merely examines a complete portfolio, which has been developed and accumulated over many years.

- *Patent clusters.* Patents may be categorized by the field of technology to which they appertain. For categorization purposes, the Patent Office classification scheme may be utilized (the Patent Office has kindly done this work for us) or any other convenient system may be employed. When plotting a number of patents in a portfolio, related categories are grouped together. It is thus theoretically possible to both identify broad areas of concentration, which would have been otherwise masked, and also determine the regions of concentration within the broader area.

- *Profiling.* Related to cluster analysis is portfolio profiling (don't worry, it raises no civil rights issues). Once a patent portfolio has been analyzed and plotted in terms of numbers of patents in various technological categories, it will be seen that the resultant plot describes the portfolio—and, by inference, the portfolio owner—in the same manner that a plot of a DNA sample describes its sample donor. By comparing such plots or "profiles," one may, theoretically, identify likely licensees, or acquisition targets, or merger partners. The critical question here, of course, is "What are we searching for—strength or weakness, similarity or dissimilarity?" The answer depends on the particular question being asked (i.e., the reason that the inquiry is being made).

- *Miscellaneous portfolio information.* It has been suggested in the literature that patent mapping may be used to highlight various features of a patent portfolio. Thus, for example, the number of patents issued in the name of various inventors may be graphed. The idea here is that the high points on the graph identify the most prolific inventors (well, duh!). It has even been suggested that this analysis be refined to identify the number of patents whose inventors are no longer employed by the patentee organization (inventor employment analysis). It is implied that having many inventors leave an organization is not a good thing (again—well, duh!). Similarly, one may graph numbers of patents against patent age. This is intended to provide an indication of portfolio aging and warn of impending expiration or technological obsolescence.

While useful, the concept of patent mapping has been somewhat oversold. It is most applicable to analysis of sizeable portfolios where it can disclose trends. It can be misleading when applied to small portfolios. Moreover, it has a significant lag time—even under the new law, patent applications are not published until 18 months after filing.

## Summary

An IP audit provides the means for taking inventory of a firm's intellectual property and assuring that all such property is properly assigned and protected. It also provides for the identification and documentation of valuable intellectual assets and corrects any shortcomings in the procedures followed by the firm in handling such assets.

A patent review committee periodically reviews the firm's patent portfolio to decide questions pertaining to the continued prosecution of patent applications, maintenance of issued patents, and the advisability of filing foreign counterpart applications.

Much information about a competitor's developments, plans and products may be gleaned from an examination of its patents. This information may be gathered by simply reviewing the *Official Patent and Trademark Gazette* or obtained from any number of service providers. Examination of competitors' patents may also give warning that one's own patents are being infringed. Patent mapping is the visual presentation of patent data.

# CHAPTER 5

# What Is It Worth—Putting a Value on Intellectual Property

## After reading this chapter, you will be able to:

- Understand the various IP valuation models
- Understand how factors such as infringement, corporate culture, national culture, and the patentee's ability to enforce patent rights can affect patent value

Having devoted such effort to creating, identifying, and protecting intellectual property, the reader is probably wondering what it is worth. (If not, the reader should be.) Certainly, venture capitalists, bankers, shareholders, and other investors—actual or potential—are asking this question.

## Valuation Models

Intellectual property, like any property, is worth what it will bring in the market. In the absence of an efficient market (a market with many buyers, many sellers and freely available information as to prices) for trading technologies, it may be quite difficult to ascertain what the market value of a particular technology may be. Nevertheless, there are several valuation models that may be employed in valuing intellectual property. Among the most widely used models are replacement cost, discounted revenue stream, market value, and incremental value.

## Replacement Cost

Replacement cost is, theoretically, what it would cost to replace the property. Although the theory is sound, the practice is weak. In practice, replacement cost is considered to be the same as development cost, although there is a theoretical difference (development cost is a historical value—what it actually cost to develop the technology at the time it was developed—while replacement cost is an estimate of what it would cost to achieve the same result now, which may be considerably different). It is, simply, the sum of the actual expenses incurred (research, development, and legal costs) in creating the property. As practiced, this method rests on the implicit assumption that the result of each dollar invested in research is equal to the result of every other dollar so spent. The fallacy of this assumption should be readily apparent to all. By this thinking, an expensive failure is worth more than an inexpensive success. However, because replacement cost is based solely upon precise, verifiable, historical data, it is dearly beloved by accountants and others of their ilk. *Do not listen to such people.*

This does not mean, however, that the replacement cost approach has no place under the sun. It does have some applicability to the valuation of trade secrets and patents. Recall that trade secrets may be legally discovered by reverse engineering or independent research. Based on

**IN THE REAL WORLD**

## An Expensive Failure

An attempt to develop a nuclear-powered aircraft was, perhaps, the most expensive R&D failure of modern times. According to the replacement cost valuation method, the end result of this failure would be worth billions of dollars (for which none would pay a dime).

this, the price of a trade secret should never exceed the cost of redis-covering it in one's own lab. Hence, the replacement cost (cost of inde-pendent development or reverse engineering) effectively places an upper limit on the value of a trade secret.

The upper value of the trade secret, in turn, is the minimum value of a patent based on the invention covered by the trade secret. Since, as previously noted (see Chapter 1), the filing of a patent application gen-erally results in a loss of the underlying trade secret pertaining to the invention, a patent applicant must be convinced that the ensuing patent will be more valuable than the lost trade secret or the patent application would not have been filed. This implicit assumption establishes the min-imum value for the patent as the cost of replacement of the underlying trade secret. Needless to say, the value of the patent could be consider-ably higher.

## Discounted Revenue Stream

The discounted revenue stream or income approach to intellectual prop-erty valuation is based on the assumption that the property will produce a stream of revenues. Obviously, if the property is licensed there will be revenues in the form of royalties. A forecast of such royalties is prepared —as to both amount and timing—and the present value of the forecast-ed stream is calculated. Clearly, the calculated value is highly dependent on the discount rate applied. However, the rate may be chosen to reflect the perceived risk and may, in this way, constitute a valuable adjustment mechanism. The capitalized revenue stream approach is best suited to sit-uations in which the property owner neither uses the underlying tech-nology nor seeks to deny its use to competitors (see Exhibit 5.1). In such circumstances, the property has no value to its owner other than the rev-enue stream it may produce. If, however, the property owner competes in the market to which the technology appertains (a word beloved by

**EXHIBIT 5.1**

# Value of Unused IP—Capitalized Revenue Stream

$$V = \sum_{i=1}^{n} \frac{R_n}{(1+I)^n}$$

Where: $V$ is the value of the subject intellectual property;
$R$ is the revenue derived from the property, i.e., royalties, in year $n$;
$I$ is the applicable discount rate chosen to reflect the risk factors; and
$n$ is the number of years in which revenue is received.

attorneys for its archaic sound), the valuation question becomes much more complex.

## Market Value

Like many people (probably including the reader), I regularly scan the notices of home sales in my community. When I find that a house similar to mine has been sold, I can assume that the value of my house is approximately equal to the sale price of the similar house. This is an example of *market valuation*. While this approach to valuation works reasonably well for valuing homes, it is difficult to apply to the valuation of patents. Since, by definition, all patented inventions are unique (well, actually "novel," but that's the same thing), it is virtually impossible to find other patents sufficiently similar to the one to be valued (in real estate, this is called *lack of comparables*). Moreover, there is no efficient market for patents—even if we could find comparables, there is no information available as to recent sales prices of such patents. In short, it works for houses, but not for patents.

assumptions. For these reasons, they are time consuming and, hence, costly to utilize.

In an effort to overcome these problems and to provide a quick and (comparatively) inexpensive means of ascertaining the value of a patent, a computerized valuation model known as TRRU$^®$ Metrics has been developed. (If an answer comes from a computer, it must be right.)

Without delving too deeply into this model, which is based on the Black-Scholes options-pricing theory, it may be said to rest on the assumptions that a patent and the patented technology are one and the same (by now, all readers should comprehend the fallacy of this assumption) and that all *technology* in a given field is of equal value, except for two factors: the investment required to bring the technology to market and the time remaining until market introduction. The TRRU$^®$ Metrics pundits have divided the technological universe into several hundred categories and, through observation of the market values assigned to companies—each of which utilizes only a single "piece" of technology (so-called pure play companies)—have determined what they consider to be the value of one piece of technology in each of their categories. The values thus determined are adjusted for the two variable factors, with the adjusted value being deemed the value of the subject "technology." Note again that no consideration has been given to any factors relating to the patent that, theoretically, determines and secures the owner's rights to the technology. The scope of the patent claims is not examined, nor its validity discussed.

Patents are not fungible. The goal is not to determine average values but, rather, the value of a specific patent.

## Mathematically Correct Patent Valuation Models

The authors will now proceed to present their own (obviously superior) valuation models. For those readers who are mathematically inclined (or simply masochistic), equations for the theoretically correct valuation of a single patent, or a portfolio of related patents, are derived, and appear in Appendix F. These formulae describe values in both a perfect world (where patents are respected, i.e., not infringed) and in the real world (where patents are routinely infringed). Models are also derived for the valuation of the individual constituents of a portfolio of related patents.

## Patent Value—A Model for a Perfect World

In nonmathematical, more generally comprehensible terms, a value is first derived for the entire portfolio of related patents—patents all directed to different aspects of a single product, or product line, or service. This value, as noted above, is defined as the difference between the revenues—sales volume multiplied by the sale price—enjoyed by the portfolio owner under exclusive conditions (this is a perfect world model) and the corresponding revenues that would result under purely competitive conditions. Summing these differences over the expected life of the patent(s) produces a value. Thus, for each period (usually, but not necessarily, these are annual periods), sales volume and the corresponding sale price must be estimated (forecasted, guessed) under both the monopolistic and competitive market assumptions. This is, of course, the weakness of the model—the calculated value is no better than the estimates on which it is based, and the estimation process itself is lengthy and tedious (it is especially suited to performance by summer interns, graduate students, and similar sources of intelligent but cheap labor). The value is found by discounting the revenue differences in succeeding years; that is to say, taking the present value of the previously calculated stream of revenue differences.

Having calculated the value of a portfolio of related patents, one can approximate the value of a single, constituent patent. First, divide the value of the entire portfolio by the number of constituent patents to calculate an average value per patent. This average value is then adjusted with regard to two factors: patent term and relative merit.

The patent term adjustment factor is essentially a fraction whose denominator is the number of periods (again, usually, but not necessarily, years) or the term over which the portfolio valuation was calculated. The denominator is the number of periods, during the valuation term, during which the subject constituent patent was active (issued and subsisting). For example, if the portfolio was valued over a five-year term, and the subject patent issued at the beginning of the third year of that term and remained subsisting (did not expire and was found neither invalid nor unenforceable by a court), the term adjustment factor would be three fifths or .6.

The relative merit adjustment is, unfortunately, more subjective. As should be apparent to the reader by this point, the relative value of the various patents in a patent portfolio is affected by the scope or breadth of the patent claims (if this is not apparent, please see Chapter 1).

## Patent Value—A Model for the Real World

The foregoing valuation model assumed that patents are universally respected—that they are not infringed (actually, it simply ignored the possibility of infringement). Unfortunately, in the real world, infringement does, sometimes (frequently), occur (it is hoped that the reader is outraged by this revelation). The question to be asked is what effect infringement has on the value of a patent or a patent portfolio. The answer to this question depends on the likelihood that the patent owner will successfully enforce the patent rights. The likelihood of successful enforcement depends on two factors: (a) the probability that the patent owner will undertake enforcement action and (b) the probability that enforcement action, undertaken by the owner, will be successful. The probability that the patent owner will seek to enforce the patent, in turn, is composed of two elements: (1) the willingness of the owner to undertake enforcement and (2) the ability to do so.

Many companies that are aware of acts of infringement of their patents are unwilling to enforce those patents for a variety of reasons. Some firms have a litigation-averse or risk-averse corporate culture. In some instances, internal corporate politics (whose department budget is going to pay for litigation?), management complacency, fear of upsetting an existing supplier or customer relationship, or fear of being accused of monopolistic behavior produce inaction, if not to say passivity.

National culture plays a role in this too. Europeans are much less likely than Americans to become engaged in patent litigation, while patent litigation is almost unheard of in Japan (and Japan is one of the largest patent filers in the world!). Needless to say, a patent portfolio owned by a company that is unlikely to enforce it is worth considerably less (if anything at all!) than a similar portfolio owned by a company that vigorously enforces its patents, all other things being equal.

The ability to enforce patents is often a matter of finance. With the median cost of patent infringement litigation approaching two million dollars, one needs to have the necessary capital before embarking on this expensive journey. Thus, a patent portfolio owned by a struggling start-up is probably worth less than a similar portfolio owned by a company with plenty of cash. A patent owned by a so-called "garage inventor" is likely to be worth even less.

If the spirit is willing, but the finances are weak, litigation may still be undertaken if one purchases an infringement abatement insurance policy, which provides—for a price (did you think insurance companies are altruistic?)—the necessary funding.

The probability of prevailing at trial is also comprised of several factors, which include: (1) the probability that at least one of the patents in the portfolio will be found to be infringed; (2) the probability that at least one of the infringed patent(s) will be found valid; and (3) the probability that at least one of the infringed and valid patent(s) will be found enforceable.

Recent research shows that the statistical probability of these values is as follows: The probability that a given patent will be found infringed is 66%. The probability that a given patent will be found valid is 67%. The probability that a given patent will be found enforceable is 88%. One cannot assume that these values are independent, as judges rule in favor of the same party on all issues in 74% of cases, and juries in 86% of cases. *In toto*, patent owners prevail 58% of the time at trial (68% in jury trials).

As stated earlier, the value of a patent portfolio does not depend on the number of constituent patents. It was also noted that this is true only in an ideal world. In the real world, where one must deal with the realities of infringement and patent enforcement, the value of a patent portfolio increases with its size. The more patents, the better.

## Summary

Various models may be employed in an effort to determine the value of a patent or a patent portfolio. The most basic, and least accurate, valuation model is replacement cost. The capitalized revenue stream is best suited to valuation of patents used exclusively as licensing vehicles.

The market value method is rarely useful for valuing intellectual property due to lack of efficient markets and the difficulty in comparing intellectual properties. The incremental value model values a patent, or patents, as the difference in value of an enterprise with the property and the value of the same enterprise without the property. The formula, also known as the excess earnings or residual value model, values all of a firm's intangibles as a whole. Although it is limited in its applicability, the

# CHAPTER 6

# Make More Money by Sharing (Licensing)

## After reading this chapter you will be able to:

- Understand why selling a patent is often a complex and difficult matter, making licensing an attractive alternative
- Properly manage a license once it's signed
- Make sure you get what the licensee has agreed to pay
- Recognize the difference between a joint venture and a strategic alliance
- Understand the choice between *paid up* and *running royalty* licenses
- Understand how to increase the value of a patent or a patent license

The question is often (but not often enough) asked: "How can we [or I, or in one instance at a cocktail party, a friend] make money from our intellectual property?" Briefly stated, there are three ways to make money from any property: (1) sell it, (2) rent it, or (3) use it. The choice depends on which approach or combination of approaches yields the greatest return.

# To Sell or Not to Sell—That Is the Question

Conceptually, the simplest way for a company to make money from intellectual property that it is not using is to sell it. The company or patent holder approaches the transaction with intellectual property and the responsibility for its maintenance and protection, and departs with money, or its equivalent (is there anything truly equivalent to money?), and no responsibilities. What could be better? Complexity, however, arises from the need to set a price. There will be only one chance to get it right.

The sale price is generally set at some fraction, typically one quarter to one half of the expected benefit to the buyer. Obviously, a problem will arise if the buyer and seller have significantly different views as to the amount of this benefit. Almost always, the benefit to be realized is proportional to the future sales of a given product or product line. These sales may be influenced by a host of factors, many of which are difficult or impossible to predict.

# Perchance to License

One way to avoid or minimize disagreements as to future benefits is to license, rather than sell, the intellectual property. If the license provides for a royalty based on actual sales of the licensed product(s)—a "running royalty"—the need to forecast future sales volumes and prices is obviated. "It is what it is" and the patent owner gets an agreed percentage of it, generally payable quarterly. Of course, this still begs the question of how to set the royalty rate. In theory, the factors that are used to determine the royalty rate of a patent license are the same factors used in setting a sale price—in essence, the royalty effects a sharing of the benefits enjoyed by the licensee by reason of the license. Thus, ideally (!), the royalty rate is set at one quarter to one half of the expected benefit. In practice, the rates tend to be at the lower end of the range.

**TIPS & TECHNIQUES**

If you haven't a clue what royalty rate to request, start with a demand for 5%, and you won't be far wrong.

As usual, however, real life is not as simple as theory. Either or both of the parties may seek to improve its position by reference to the royalty rates of other existing licenses, the implicit assumption being that the rates in these other licenses are somehow relevant to the question of the appropriate rate for the license at issue. Thus, for example, licensors will generally point to the royalty rates in licenses they had previously granted under the same patents. This, in fact, has some relevancy. Either party may argue about "typical" or "standard in the industry" rates (the terms in quotations are often euphemisms for "unverifiable"). This, in fact, is largely irrelevant. Licensees may occasionally point to the royalty rates in other licenses they have taken, or licenses they have granted. This, in fact, is completely irrelevant, if not totally inane.

## It Ain't Over Till It's Over

Many patentees believe that the battle is over when a license is finally executed. Wrong! After a license is executed, it must be policed. First and foremost, is the licensee timely making all royalty payments required under the license agreement? Note that the foregoing is a compound question (lawyerspeak for unfair or tricky); let's parse it (heck, Bill Clinton could parse "is"):

- Timely—was payment received in the allotted time?
- All—were all sales covered by the license reported?
- Made—were all required payments actually received?

A surprising number of licensors file away (and forget) their executed licenses without docketing scheduled payments. *Do not do this.* Some licensees, for example, forget to make their quarterly royalty payments. It is up to the licensor to provide a *written* reminder when a payment is overdue. This, of course, requires that the licensor knows when a payment is overdue.

Not all licensees report all licensed sales (surprise!). Keep track of all licensees' payments. Does the current payment seem unusual as compared to past payments, or the payments of other licensees? If a licensee claims business is poor, check the licensee's web site. Is the licensee boasting to the world about how business is expanding? Check sales reported by licensees with purchases of their known customers. Are there any inconsistencies? If the licensee is a public company, peruse their 10Q filings. What are they telling their shareholders?

Licenses should include a provision allowing the licensor to audit the books of a licensee to the extent of verifying the accuracy of the licensee's reports of sales of licensed goods. Such audit provisions should provide that the licensee will bear the cost of an audit if a material discrepancy—usually 5% or more of the amount properly due—is discovered. Audits can be rather costly ($5,000 to $10,000) and therefore are not to be undertaken lightheartedly. Often, however, the mere threat of an audit will produce the desired result—the licensee discovers an unfortunate error, and tenders a check (sometimes with apologies, sometimes without).

Monitor the licensee's product literature (most often, this is available on the licensee's web site). Are there any new products, or new models of old products, that are subject to the terms of the license but are not being reported (and for which no royalties are being paid)? In this regard, it may be advantageous to include an arbitration provision in a license, whereby any dispute as to whether a new product is subject to the license may be (reasonably) promptly and inexpensively resolved.

Finally, demand periodic verification that the licensee is complying with the patent marking and any similar provisions of the license. (If this doesn't seem familiar, for shame!—see Chapter 1).

## Nothing Ventured, Nothing Gained

The situation may arise that the owner of intellectual property wishes to capitalize on this property, yet lacks an essential element to do so. For example, the property owner may have insufficient manufacturing capacity, or may lack an effective distribution system. The property owner may believe that marketing muscle, in the form of a well-recognized trademark or service mark, would be necessary to get the new product (or service) off the ground. If another firm can supply the missing element, a *joint venture* may be an effective vehicle for commercializing the property.

Basically, a joint venture is an entity, such as a partnership or corporation, created for a specific limited purpose and owned by two or more parties. The contributions or investments of each of the joint venturers (owners) are usually in kind, not in cash. In this instance, the intellectual property owner would contribute the intellectual property, either by assignment or license, while the other venturers would, perhaps, contribute appropriate manufacturing or distribution services and a trademark or service mark (again, either by assignment or license). Hopefully, the whole is greater than the sum of its parts.

Because a joint venture is a separate entity, it allows its owners to continue their own existence with minimal interference. The joint venture is most often dissolved when its purpose is accomplished. For this reason, it is especially important that the parties agree, during its formation, upon a plan of termination, including the question of ownership of any intellectual property created by the joint venture itself.

A strategic alliance primarily differs from a joint venture in that it is not a separate entity. Rather, it is simply an agreement between its various members (the allies) to cooperate in some specified manner. Generally, the allies offer each other preferential, or exclusive, terms with respect to the sale of goods or the provision of services. The goods or services subject to the agreement most commonly are those in which the supplier enjoys some competitive advantage. The alliances are constituted so that each member receives, under most favorable terms, those goods or services it needs to enable it to most effectively capitalize upon its own area of strength or comparative advantage. Because it is not an entity, a strategic alliance cannot develop or hold intellectual property. For this reason, dissolution or expiration of a strategic alliance presents few of the problems inherent in the termination of a joint venture.

## Risk and Price—Package Deals in IP Licensing

Businesspeople, as a rule, prefer to avoid or minimize risk. Given a choice, they gravitate toward those investments or projects that involve the least uncertainty. Obviously, the prospect of a large reward may tempt people to accept risk; but, as between different investments offering similar potential rewards, the one perceived as presenting the least risk will be the most popular and, hence, will command the highest price. This principle lies at the heart of the franchising industry.

Franchise purchasers pay a substantial premium over the costs they would otherwise incur in starting a similar business *ab initio* (the Latin is so much more impressive than the corresponding "from scratch"). What does the franchise purchaser receive in exchange for this premium? Greater certainty—as much as anything can be certain in business. The franchisee receives detailed specifications, formulae, and process directions for the products or services that the new business will offer. Lists of suppliers are also provided, as is training for employees. All necessary equipment and tools arrive in a package. Frequently, the franchisor includes assistance with such things as site selection, application for necessary permits and approvals, and establishing accounting and other control systems. Moreover, and most importantly, the franchise includes a license under the franchisor's trademarks.

The same principle applies to intellectual property licensing. It is, most certainly, possible to assign or license a patent, for example, without offering anything more. Such transactions, however, are generally in the nature of patent enforcement actions. In these instances, a matter of patent infringement is (more or less) amicably resolved when the infringer acquires the infringed patent, or a license thereunder (so-called "stick licensing"). Such a license engenders little technological risk—the infringing product is already on the market. Indeed, by taking a license, the former infringer actually reduces its risk, by eliminating the risk of being sued for patent infringement.

Quite a different situation results, however, when a party is not already using the patented technology. In such a case, the party is under no compulsion to acquire the patent or take a license. Adoption of a new—and therefore untested and unproven—technology presents substantial risks. The technology may prove to be flawed. It may require further (expensive) development before it is ready for the market. Even if there are no technological problems, or if such problems are successfully solved, the technology may still fail in the market for any of a variety of reasons. The greater the perceived risk associated with a new technology, the greater the reluctance to invest substantial resources to acquire and commercialize it and, as a result, the lower the price the technology can command. Once this relationship between price and risk is recognized, the solution becomes obvious: Reduce the risk associated with a technology, and the price it commands will increase.

Risk reduction is, in essence, a matter of providing solutions to those problems that would otherwise constitute risks. Just as a franchisee willingly pays a premium for a "turnkey" business operation, so too will a prospective assignee or licensee pay a premium for a market-ready or market-proven technology. In other words, a tested and proven new product or service, covered by a patent, will fetch a much higher price than the patent alone. Therefore, whenever possible, sell a product, not a patent. Package the patent with applicable trademarks, design specifications, blueprints, test results, process know-how, quality assurance procedures, lists of qualified suppliers, market research data, and anything else that will facilitate commercialization of the patented technology. Such information is of value to a prospective buyer in two respects: It reduces the additional investment required to achieve commercialization, and it reduces the risk of failure. It is comparatively easy to sell a successful product or service. The closer an invention is to market—the fewer the remaining problems—the more it will bring. Moreover, a package license, including trademarks and know-how, may continue generating royalties after the patents in the package have expired.

Since (some) patents have value, they may, under appropriate circumstances, be used as collateral for loans. While most banks still refuse to make loans collateralized solely by patents, there are now certain specialized (and more enlightened) financial institutions, such as Licent Capital, LLC, that will do so.

**IN THE REAL WORLD**

## The Odds Against an Inventor

Only about 1 patent in 20 is licensed, and only about 1 in 100 patents generates any royalties.

# The Carrot and the Stick

Two terms commonly used (actually, overused) in the licensing business are *carrot license* and *stick license*. For this reason and no other, the authors feel compelled to explain them.

In plain English, a carrot license is a voluntary license, while a stick license is taken under duress. Generally, an infringer or an accused infringer takes the stick license in settlement of a lawsuit, or under threat of one. Thus, a stick license should be viewed as a patent enforcement tool. (A stick license is an offer you can't refuse; a carrot license is one you can.)

Although the meaning of the term *carrot license* is clear, the underlying concept is barren. Virtually no one comes knocking on a licensor's door, hat and checkbook in hand, politely inquiring about the availability and cost of a license. As a practical matter, convincing a noninfringer to take a patent license is a tough job, consisting, as it does, of two parts: (1) convincing the party that they *want* to use the patented technology, and then (2) convincing them that they have to *pay* for it. The first part essentially consists of the tasks of finding a party that actually could benefit from the use of the technology, and then overcoming the natural reluctance of that party to adopt technology from outside (the infamous "not invented here" syndrome). Upon successfully completing the first task, the prospective licensor must then convince the party that unlicensed use will be vigorously ("sue the sucker") opposed. Thus, even a carrot license has elements of the stick.

# Summary

There are three ways to make money from a patent: use it, rent (license) it, or sell (assign) it. The sale price of a patent is typically one quarter to one half of the expected benefit to the buyer. Ideally, a royalty in a license effects a similar sharing of the benefit derived from the use of the patented technology. Royalties may be paid in a lump sum—a "paid up" license—or may be based on sales of the licensed products—a "running royalty." Once a license has been executed, it should be policed to ensure that all payments are made in a timely manner and in the proper amount.

The price that a patent or a patent license may command is often increased if the patent is packaged with corresponding know-how and other information that facilitates commercialization of the patented technology by the assignee or licensee.

# Officers and Directors Beware—You Can Be Liable for Mismanaging Intellectual Property

## After reading this chapter you will be able to:

- Understand the responsibilities of corporate officers and directors with respect to the management of intellectual property and the extent to which such responsibilities may be delegated

- Understand the liabilities that may attach to corporate officers and directors who fail to satisfy their duty of care with respect to the management of intellectual property or are responsible for acts of infringement

- Develop a program to satisfy officers' and directors' intellectual property management responsibilities

Recent changes in the value and role of intellectual property present the business corporation with newfound opportunities; however, they also expose its officers and directors to newfound risks and potential liabilities. In times past, directors and senior officers could—and almost universally did—ignore intellectual property, leaving it to a clerical staff who filed and forgot it. It was a rare company indeed where the intellectual property portfolio was accorded a fraction of the attention directed to tangible assets. Now, however, the increased importance of the intellectual property portfolio mandates a commensurate increase in the care with which it is managed. It must, in fact, be managed with the same degree of care and attention as is devoted to the company's tangible assets. Failure to meet this new standard may well have serious legal implications for the firm's officers and directors.

## Nature of Injuries Arising from Mismanagement of Intellectual Property

Every officer and director of a corporation, as a fiduciary, has an affirmative duty of care, which is, broadly stated, a responsibility to diligently manage the affairs and assets of the corporation, and to consider the possible ramifications of its action (or inaction).

The business laws of the state in which the business is incorporated govern the duty of care and any liability arising thereunder. Aside from any liability arising under state statutes related to the duty of care, the officers and directors of publicly traded companies may also incur liability under federal securities laws.

Injuries arising from the mismanagement or nonmanagement of intellectual property fall, most commonly, into two general categories: waste and misvaluation.

Waste occurs when an asset is not utilized, or not utilized fully, or is sold for much less than its true value. Avoidance of waste of intellectual property requires, among other things, identification of all of its possible uses and the estimated extent of such uses, determination of the existence and merits of competing technologies, and where a patent is involved, assessment of the strength of the patent and the scope of its claims.

Patents protecting unused technology are a prime example of unutilized assets. Failure to license such unused intellectual property and produce an income stream may be a waste of corporate assets, which may expose officers and directors to liability.

Novel technology is an asset. The failure to aggressively patent the results of corporate research and development (R&D), like the failure to insure valuable plant and equipment, may be deemed mismanagement. Most U.S. companies face a dilemma of whether to obtain foreign patents or trademarks, in addition to their U.S. rights, and in which countries to seek such protection.

Failure to enforce intellectual property rights is another example of mismanagement of corporate assets. Many technology-related corporations are rushing to file as many patents as possible, which may or may not be a prudent strategy. However, patents afford only exclusionary rights. Failure to enforce these rights by bringing a patent infringement action creates a double waste: loss of a valuable monopoly on the use of the patented technology as well as a waste of the capital spent on obtaining and maintaining the unenforced patents. Furthermore, any delay in enforcing the infringed patents may result in laches and estoppel (see Chapter 8), which may ultimately reduce the damage awards when an action is brought at a later date or render the patents unenforceable. Therefore, there may well be an affirmative duty on corporate officers and directors to vigorously enforce corporate intellectual property rights in a timely manner.

Although it causes different injuries, misvaluation is closely related to waste. Where waste can be described as a *realized* loss, misvaluation is a

**IN THE REAL WORLD**

## Oops!

It has been estimated that nearly 40% of the market valuation of the average company is missing from its balance sheet.

*book* loss. Both spring from the same errors and omissions. Misvalued intellectual property can adversely affect the total valuation of the transaction in a merger, acquisition, divestiture, or equity financing.

Failure to communicate the value of the intellectual property of a publicly traded company to the financial community may result in undervalued stock, thus causing loss of value to shareholders. Such issues, for example, as a patent, newly issued to a competitor, which may be infringed by the company's product, need to be disclosed to shareholders, regardless of whether actual infringement notice has been given. Reasonable apprehension of a possible patent infringement lawsuit should be disclosed, as should the expiration dates of important patents, which may adversely affect the company's market share. Such disclosures may need to be made in press releases, in annual and quarterly financial statements, and in the Management Discussion and Analysis section of registered financial statements filed with the Securities and Exchange Commission (SEC). Failure to accurately and timely report information relevant to corporate intellectual property to the shareholders, in the initial prospectus as well as in quarterly and annual reports, may result in their ill-advised decision making and subsequent losses, prompting them to seek relief in a class-action suit against the officers and directors.

## Standard of Responsibility for Portfolio Management

Waste by not (or under-) exploiting corporate intellectual property assets need not involve any wrongdoing or evil intent, such as would incur criminal liability. It may be merely negligent; a proverbial sin of omission. Negligent waste may be established by a showing that no person of ordinary sound business judgment would say that a fair benefit had been derived from the challenged transaction. In this regard, it must be borne in mind that intellectual property is almost always a wasting asset—patents expire, technology becomes obsolete. Thus, waste may result from any or all of the following:

- Inadequacy of return for the license or sale of intellectual property
- Failure to utilize intellectual property
- Undue narrowness of its utilization
- Undue utilization delay

While there is no relevant case law specifically dealing with mismanagement of corporate intellectual property assets, there is no reason to believe that the standards the courts will apply for directors' and officers' responsibility for management of intellectual property assets will differ from the well-established criteria and standards for duty of care in managing other corporate assets. Until relatively recently, the market for technology stocks moved spectacularly and consistently upward and everyone was a "winner." With the recent market downturn (or collapse), however, it seems only a matter of time until some disgruntled shareholders of a publicly traded technology company, having seen their stock price plummet or the company dissolved in bankruptcy, will attempt to recoup their losses in a derivative class-action suit against officers and directors for mismanaging corporate intellectual property assets. Directors and officers of publicly traded companies are well advised to take prudent steps today to protect themselves from future liability.

One of the factors considered in determining whether a firm's officers and directors have met their duty of care with respect to management of the firm's intellectual property is the nature of the company's business. Thus, it has been held that a director's duty may be greater where the company engages in a business implicating the general public, especially where there is an established regulatory scheme for such business. Chief among such businesses is banking, including investment banking. Bank officers and directors are typically held to a higher standard than the officers and directors of other businesses. While IP portfolio valuation is always a prudent step in the management of corporate assets, obtaining an opinion as to the value of an IP portfolio involved in an initial public offering (IPO), merger and acquisition (M&A), divestiture, or corporate reorganization may be considered virtually obligatory. (Although the legal standard applied by courts to publicly traded companies may be the same as privately held nonbanking concerns, the SEC itself is a powerful potential plaintiff whose mere presence can have a marked, chilling effect.) As expected, in determining what would be prudent under similar circumstances, the courts look to the practices and procedures of similar businesses; and a failure to adopt such practices and follow such procedures as are accepted as necessary by the officers and directors of similar businesses is almost invariably held to establish negligence.

Therefore, should the directors and officers of other high-tech companies expect to be held to the standards of IBM, which generates over $1 billion a year in licensing revenues? Probably not. They are certainly well advised, however, to look into adopting some of the IP management strategies employed by IBM, Texas Instruments, Dow Chemical, and a number of other standard-setting companies.

Typically (when all other avenues of escape are blocked), officers and directors seek to defend their acts (or, more often, their omissions) on the basis of the *business judgment rule*. The courts, however, have begun to more clearly invoke the threshold requirement that the challenged decision must have resulted from the exercise of *informed business judgment*, based on all information *reasonably available*. A reasonable investigation is generally deemed necessary to satisfy this requirement.

Acceptance or rejection of a settlement offer in patent infringement litigation, for example, is a decision—if made on an informed basis—that can be justified under the business judgment rule. If, however, the management and the board fail to analyze the litigation risk and consider other relevant factors, they may be exposed to potentially serious liability in the event the litigation results in an unfavorable judgment and a substantial loss.

Finally, it is to be noted that the acceptance of the office of a director implies a competent knowledge of the duties assumed. A director cannot be excused for imprudence on the grounds of ignorance or inexperience. Serving without compensation or merely as an accommodation does not negate the director's responsibilities.

While the burden of proof to establish officers and directors liable for waste is a heavy one, the question is, nonetheless, one of fact. Thus, in the absence of substantial justification for challenged transactions, one accused of waste may well be forced to face the perils and uncertainty of trial.

## Delegation of Responsibility

While responsibility for management of the IP portfolio may be delegated, such delegation must comply with certain requirements if it is to satisfy the duties of the corporate officers and directors. A director's ability to delegate responsibility to nondirectors is essentially limited to activities that are in the ordinary and usual course of business. The director should, despite any delegation, remain informed as to the policies and affairs of the corporation and maintain a general knowledge of the employment of the corporation's resources. He is chargeable with knowledge that he might have possessed had he diligently discharged his functions and, thus, is presumed to know everything concerning corporate affairs that he might have learned by the exercise of reasonable care and diligence. Where the duty of knowing facts exists, ignorance due to neglect of duty may create the same liability as actual knowledge and a failure to act on that knowledge.

Where a board of directors appoints a committee of its members to assume responsibility for a task, a nonmember director is expected to still comply with the standard of care in satisfying himself that the committee, upon which he proposes to rely, reasonably merits his confidence. This would require, as appropriate, that he generally familiarize himself with the investigative or other activities of the committee. Moreover, neither the designation of such a committee, the delegation of authority to the committee, nor the action of the committee pursuant to such authority alone constitutes full compliance by any nonmember director with his duties as a director.

One measure often taken by directors is to seek the advice of experts. Indeed, relevant precedent suggests that failure to seek advice from outside experts may, in some circumstances, itself constitute a breach of the duty to be informed. There are a number of IP management firms providing businesses with such expert advice. Where directors seek expert advice and honestly act under it, they are protected from personal liability, even though the advice ultimately proves erroneous. In order to be entitled to rely on an expert's report, statement, or opinion, the director must have read it or have been present at a meeting in which it was orally presented, or have taken other steps to become generally familiar with its contents.

## Liability for Failure to Meet Duty of Care

Where an officer or director fails to meet his duty of care, and a waste of the corporation's intellectual property assets results from that failure, that officer or director may be personally liable of the loss suffered. One or more of the shareholders or the directors may bring an action, on behalf of the corporation, to recover the damages. Under some statutes, officers and directors may be held liable to corporate creditors for losses suffered as a result of their mismanagement. If the corporation is in reorganization or liquidation, the corporation's trustees or receivers may bring an action against negligent officers or directors. A director of a holding company may be liable to that company for the diminished value of its shares resulting from his or her waste of intellectual property assets of a subsidiary company, even though he or she might also be liable to the subsidiary corporation for the same act.

Misrepresentation or omission of material information pertaining to the intellectual property of the issuer of securities may be a violation of Section 10(b) of the Securities Exchange Act of 1934, as is presentation of values for IP assets that are based on invalid data or techniques. Further, decline in the price of stock resulting from the dissemination of false information as to the value of corporate IP assets constitutes a direct, and hence actionable, injury to individual shareholders. Repeatedly, the courts have held that the failure to determine the actual (as opposed to book) value of a corporation engaged in a merger is a breach of the director's duty of care. Intangible IP assets are a major factor contributing to the discrepancy between the actual and the book value of an enterprise. Moreover, where directors did not make reasonable inquiry into the methods used to value a corporation's assets, their decisions were not entitled to the beneficial presumption of the business judgment rule.

## What to Do

Intellectual property and its management can no longer be relegated to middle management or even to an in-house patent counsel overburdened with filing and prosecuting patent applications. It must be addressed by corporate directors and officers. Despite the obvious complexities involved, they should devise and establish a reasonable IP management program and make reasonable inquiries and keep diligently informed as to the implementation of such a program.

An IP portfolio audit (see Chapter 4) is a necessary first step to avoid waste of the enterprise's assets. Prudence would dictate that a specialist manager and/or IP management firm be retained to perform such an audit and to otherwise manage a corporation's IP portfolio. The advisability of this course of action is highlighted by the growing presence and acceptance of such firms. As the employment of such firms becomes more widespread, it may have the effect, as previously noted, of raising the standards to which others are held. Thus, there is a strong impetus to jump on the bandwagon. Given the higher standards to which bankers are traditionally held, this advice should apply with even greater force to investment bankers and underwriters.

In choosing a manager or management firm, certain criteria should apply if reliance on their advice is to be deemed reasonable. Obviously, the individual(s) involved must have appropriate education and experience, particularly in the field of IP management, IP law, and the technologies of interest to the corporation. There should be a documented history of success in the management of intellectual property. Further, the chosen manager(s) should be required to provide regular and complete reports of their activities, including reasonably detailed descriptions of methodologies employed.

## Damned If You Don't, Damned If You Do

Not only may corporate officers and directors be held liable for their mismanagement of the firm's IP—generally acts of negligence or omission—they may also, under certain circumstances, be held personally liable for the company's acts of patent infringement.

Many officers and directors believe (profess to believe, try to believe, wish to believe, or in some cases, pretend to believe) that personal liability will attach only if there is a "piercing of the corporate veil." Piercing of the corporate veil is a legal doctrine that permits the court to disregard the existence of the corporation and proceed against individual officers and directors, if this is necessary to prevent (among other evils) fraud, injustice, or a thwarting of public policy. As a practical matter, the doctrine is applied when the corporation is inadequately capitalized, has failed to comply with organizational formalities, or is being used for fraudulent purposes. Efforts to pierce the veil are rarely successful. Thus, the belief in the invulnerability of officers and directors was, in most cases, well founded. This has now changed.

The Court of Appeals for the Federal Circuit (CAFC) has now held (*Hoover Group Inc. v. Custom Metalcraft, Inc.,* 94-1285 [Fed. Cir. 1996]) that it is not necessary to pierce the corporate veil in order that a person in a control position be held personally liable for the tortuous acts of the corporation (patent infringement being a tortuous act). Rather, the court is to consider several factors, including the nature of the wrongdoing, the culpability of the act (and the actor), and whether the person sought to be held personally responsible acted in his own interest or the interest of the corporation (in some small, owner-managed businesses, the two are the same). In many cases, this new standard is more encompassing than the old one. Thus, the corporate charter may no longer be proof against all attacks on those in control positions—one more good reason for officers and directors to exercise reasonable care in patent matters.

## Summary

Intellectual property must be managed with the same degree of care and caution as is devoted to a firm's tangible assets. Injuries arising from mismanagement of IP generally fall into two categories: waste and misvaluation.

The standard of care demanded of corporate officers and directors may be more stringent where the company engages in a business, such as banking, that implicates the general public.

In determining whether an action or decision was prudent, the courts generally look to the practices and procedures of similar businesses; failure to adopt such practices and procedures is almost invariably held to be negligent.

A corporate director may delegate his responsibilities with respect to IP management, but must still remain informed as to such affairs.

Personal liability may result where an officer or director fails to meet his duty of care and a waste of the corporation's IP assets results. Such liability may be to the corporation itself, the shareholders, and, in some circumstances, to creditors and trustees or receivers. Where there is a failure to disclose material information pertaining to intellectual property, or if such information is misrepresented, criminal liability may attach.

Prudence suggests that directors retain a qualified specialist manager and/or an IP management firm to perform an audit and to manage the firm's IP portfolio.

It is no longer necessary to pierce the corporate veil to find officers and directors personally liable for acts of patent infringement committed by the corporation. Instead, the court will examine the personal culpability of the individuals involved.

# CHAPTER 8

# Enforcing Your Rights

## After reading this chapter you will be able to:

- Understand the types of infringement (literal and under the doctrine of equivalents)

- Know the importance of having the broadest possible claims coverage when drafting a patent application

- Understand the ramifications of the *Festo* case for patentees

- Choose the best venue for your litigation

- Communicate with patent infringers in the most effective (and least self-defeating) way

- Anticipate an infringer's preemptive strike—the declaratory judgment action

- Understand the two kinds of damages (lost profits and reasonable royalty) that may be awarded in a patent infringement case and the requirements for each

- Understand the role of convoyed sales in assessing a reasonable royalty

- Understand the usual path of patent litigation and some factors that contribute to the individuality of each particular case

- Understand two common defenses, laches and estoppel, and the differences between them

- Prepare a quantitative analysis of litigation risk
- Choose a law firm to represent you in litigation matters
- Protect yourself against overbilling by your law firm
- Identify which infringer(s) to sue first and which defendants will be the most aggressive
- Determine if pendant claims are also involved in a company's infringement of your patent
- Present a positive image of your company to a jury
- Understand reexamination and the issues regarding its use
- Understand the advantages of settlement as opposed to litigation
- Understand the forms of alternative dispute resolution, along with their benefits and drawbacks

# Patent Infringement

## Patent Claims—Where Less Is More

The scope of a patent is determined by its claims. If each and every limitation of a claim is found in an accused device or process, the claim is said to *read on* that device or process and is infringed thereby. If a single limitation is missing from the accused structure, there is no infringement (this requirement is known as the *all elements rule*). However, the presence of additional features in the accused structure does not negate infringement.

Not infrequently (only lawyers and politicians talk like that—in double negatives), an inventor reviewing a draft of a patent application prior to filing will complain that lots of things were left out of the claims. This is not an error or failure on the part of the patent practitioner. It is, in fact, a measure of the practitioner's skill (assuming the claim is, ultimately, allowed by the patent examiner). The goal of the practitioner is (or at least should be) to secure the broadest possible claims coverage. This is accomplished by drafting patent claims with the fewest possible limitations. Each limitation in a patent claim is a potential avenue to claim circumvention. The greater the number of limitations in a patent claim, the greater the probability that the subject invention can be substantially copied or imitated, while one claim limitation is omitted. If this occurs, the copy does not infringe the patent claim—remember the all elements rule. When reviewing a draft patent application, object to patent claims that appear too detailed, not to those that appear too general.

Infringement may be either literal or under the doctrine of equivalents. *Literal infringement* occurs when the claim language literally reads on the accused device or process. If, however, one or more claim limitations are not literally met by the accused device, all may not be lost.

In order to prevent the perpetration of a fraud on the patent—circumvention of the patent by means of a trivial change or modification—the courts long ago created the *doctrine of equivalents.* Under this doctrine (which, as you will see, is subject to a number of limitations), if a claim limitation is not literally met, but the corresponding structure in the accused device, or the corresponding step in the accused process, "performs substantially the same function, in substantially the same way, to achieve the same result," the claim may still be infringed. Note that the doctrine is applied on a limitation-by-limitation basis, not on the basis of an entire claim.

The chief limitation on the interpretation or construction of words or phrases in a patent claim is *file wrapper estoppel,* a doctrine created by the courts that prevents a patentee from recapturing, through a broad interpretation of words or phrases in a claim, that which was previously surrendered in securing allowance of the claim. Thus, the scope of a patent claim is largely determined by the prosecution history of the patent (i.e., the file wrapper).

## The *Festo* Case: You May Not Have What You Thought You Had

Charles Dickens created the ghost of Christmas past, which haunted Ebenezer Scrooge for his past acts of avarice. The Court of Appeals for the Federal Circuit (CAFC) has created *Festo* (*Festo Corp. v. Shoketsu Kinzoku Kogyo Kabushiki Co., Ltd.*, 234 F.3d 558 [Fed. Cir. 2000]), which haunts patentees for their past acts of claim amendment committed during the prosecution of their patent applications.

Patent claims are to be written so as to apprise the reader of the precise limits of that in which the patentee claims an exclusive right (the so-called notice requirement). When infringement is literal, this notice requirement is rather easily satisfied. When infringement is founded on the doctrine of equivalents, however, the clarity of a claim becomes less certain. The range of equivalents to be accorded a claim limitation was traditionally determined—more precisely, limited—by the doctrine of file wrapper estoppel. Thus, traditionally, an analysis of the scope of a patent claim necessitated a review of the file wrapper and a detailed analysis of the estoppels (if any) created by each and every amendment made to the patent claims during prosecution. This was a complex task, even for experienced professionals.

Enter the CAFC, eager to reduce complexity and restore clarity to claim construction. Seizing the opportunity presented by the *Festo* case, the court, overturning lengthy and substantial precedent, decided, essentially on policy grounds, that the necessity for identifying and analyzing file wrapper estoppels was inimical to the requirement of claim clarity. The solution they chose was to simply eliminate *all* equivalents of any claim limitation that had been amended during prosecution. No need to analyze the extent of an estoppel—if a limitation had been amended, henceforth, it had no equivalents. The limitation would now be construed to cover that which had been disclosed in the patent specification and no more. Simple but deadly. With the stroke of a pen (or a word processor), the court had narrowed the scope of tens of thousands of subsisting patents—patents that had been prosecuted in reliance on a body of law now suddenly, and retroactively, reversed. Approximately 1.2 million currently subsisting patents include claims that were amended during prosecution and are, therefore, affected by this decision.

Dickens allowed Ebenezer to escape the haunting by reforming (actually, old Eb overreacted by becoming a spendthrift). The CAFC offers patentees no such escape. Salvation will occur only when the Supreme Court, which has recently granted certiorari (arcane terminology meaning they agreed to consider the matter), drives a stake through its heart and lays it to rest. At present, one can only hope for such an exorcism. In the meantime, various prosecution tactics are being proposed in an effort to deal with the (as yet unclear) effects of the decision. While the efficacy of these tactics is yet to be determined, the universal result (surprise!) is to vastly increase the costs of patent prosecution.

## Partners in Crime—Contributory Infringement and Inducing Infringement

A party who, without authorization, practices the patented invention of another, is a direct infringer. There are circumstances, however, that may render it difficult—if not economically impractical—to sue the direct infringer(s) of a patent. Suppose, for example, that you have a patent on a new and improved water-based paint. Suppose further that an odious and unprincipled paint manufacturer mixes all of the ingredients of this new paint, save only the water, and sells the dry mix to consumers who take it home and mix it with water, thereby completing the production of the patented paint. Clearly, each of these consumers is a direct infringer of the patent. However, while there are many of these infringers, each one has produced only a small amount of paint. It would be extremely difficult, if not impossible, to identify them; and, if they were identified, the amount of damages recoverable from any one of them is far less than the costs of even uncontested litigation. Does this mean that you are without an effective remedy? No! The paint manufacturer is a contributory infringer and, under the law (35 USC, 271(c)), is liable for all of the direct infringement resulting from his sale of the dry mix. A contributory infringer is one who sells, offers to sell, or imports into the United States a component that is a material part of a patented invention, knowing that the component is especially made or adapted for use in an infringement of the patent where the component is not a staple item having a substantial noninfringing use.

Note that it is not necessary that the seller actually know of the existence of the patent that is being infringed, merely that he or she know of the use to which his or her components will be put.

Assume now that the dry paint mix could also be combined with linseed oil, in place of water, to produce an oil-based paint. This would be a substantial noninfringing use. In such case, the paint manufacturer would not be a contributory infringer.

Finally, assume that the owner of the paint store where the dry mix is sold recommends to purchasers of the mix that they combine it with water. The paint store owner is inducing infringement and, under the law (35 USC 271(b)), is liable for all of the direct infringement resulting from his or her ill-advised recommendation.

The lesson here is this: Whenever there occurs an epidemic of infringement of a patent, look for one who is inducing the infringement or contributing to it. If such a party is found, sue the sucker.

# Risks of Patent Litigation

Every grab for the brass ring carries the risk that you will fall off the merry-go-round. This also holds true for patent litigation.

In order to *prevail*, a patentee must establish that the patent-in-suit is infringed, and must also successfully defend that patent against any defense (almost certain to be raised) of invalidity and/or unenforceability. To *succeed*, the patentee must also recover damages in an amount appreciably in excess of the costs of litigation.

## Invalidity

A patent enjoys a presumption of validity unless found by a court to be invalid. A patent may be found to be invalid for several reasons. An accused infringer will inevitably search the prior art in an effort to find pertinent references not considered by the Patent and Trademark Office when the patent was granted. The extent of such a search is limited only by the determination of the accused infringer and, faced with a potential liability for tens of millions of dollars in damages, such a party can be very determined indeed. Newly discovered prior art may establish that the claimed invention lacks novelty or would have been obvious to one of ordinary skill in the art at the time the invention was made. Although a more difficult defense, the accused may also seek to establish that the inventor has concealed the best mode of practicing the invention or that the patent is not enabling (see Chapter 1). An infringer may establish that the patent application had been filed more than a year after the patented product was introduced in the marketplace. Moreover, if the infringer can prove to the court that the patentee had concealed relevant prior art from the Patent Office (i.e., engaged in inequitable conduct), the patent may be declared unenforceable (i.e., good for nothing).

## Noninfringement

It may be found that the accused product does not infringe the patent-in-suit. In this regard, two recent cases have tipped the scales of justice in favor of the defendant.

The Supreme Court, in the famous (or, depending on one's point of view, infamous) *Markman* decision (*Markman v. Westview Instruments, Inc.*, 52 F.3d 967 [Fed. Cir. 1995] aff'd 116 S.Ct. 1384 [1996]), held that patent claims are to be construed (i.e., interpreted) by the court (the judge) as a matter of law (more on this later). To perform this function, the trial judge holds what has come to be known as a Markman hearing. After both sides have submitted proposed constructions of any disputed patent claim terms, the judge hears arguments, examines the patent and its file wrapper (see how important the file wrapper is?), and issues a decision. Except in very rare cases, expert testimony or other extrinsic evidence is not admitted. Once the court has construed the patent claims, it is often clear to both sides whether the claims, as construed, are literally infringed. The claim constructions adapted by the trial judge tend to be narrower than those that would have been adopted under similar circumstances by a jury.

As noted earlier, the *Festo* case has effectively eliminated the doctrine of equivalents with respect to any claim limitation that was amended during the course of prosecution of the patent. There is a real probability (hope, prayer, supplication) that the Supreme Court will overturn this decision; but, unless and until this occurs, the effective scope of many patents has been severely reduced.

## Avoiding Pyrrhic Victories

For reasons that will soon become apparent, patent infringement litigation is very costly. The costs of litigation, except in rather rare circumstances, are *not* awarded to the prevailing party. Thus, as a general rule, a patentee should not undertake litigation unless the expected or probabilistic recovery, including damages and the value of a permanent injunction barring further infringement, substantially exceeds the anticipated litigation costs (more about this shortly). Attorney's fees may be awarded to a prevailing patentee, in a so-called exceptional case, when it is found that the infringer lacked a good faith belief in its defenses or otherwise raised meritless or frivolous defenses. Similarly, however, the case may be found to be exceptional where the patent-in-suit is found to be invalid or unenforceable for reasons known to the patentee. In such event, litigation costs may be awarded to the defendant. Generally, this occurs when the patentee has:

- Concealed a known prior art reference from the patent examiner (inequitable conduct)
- Concealed the best mode of practicing the patented invention
- Failed to disclose a prior sale, offer for sale, public use, or description in a written publication (statutory bars)
- Misused the patent in a tying arrangement
- Sought to enforce it beyond its term

Indeed, seeking to enforce a patent known to be invalid, or otherwise misusing a patent, may itself be an antitrust violation, exposing the offending patentee to counterclaims and possible multiple damages.

## Jurisdiction and Venue— Location, Location, Location

In military science, much weight is accorded the advantages conferred by fighting a battle on ground of one's own choosing. In litigation, much weight is accorded the advantages conferred by trying the case in a courtroom of one's own choosing. A plaintiff, however, does not have complete freedom in deciding where to sue. The available choices are limited by the twin requirements of jurisdiction and proper venue.

Jurisdiction is of two kinds. Subject matter jurisdiction is the authority of the court to hear (try) cases of a particular type. Personal jurisdiction is the authority of a court to exercise control over a particular defendant. Proper venue is, similarly, that court, or courts, among all those having jurisdiction, where the case properly (elegant term meaning "according to the rules provided for such matters") may be heard. The federal courts have exclusive jurisdiction over patent and copyright infringement matters, meaning that any such case can be brought only in federal court.

Personal jurisdiction is conferred on a court by residence or, in some circumstances, by the actions of a party. Thus, a court has personal jurisdiction over any party that resides within its district. Moreover, if a non-resident party commits acts having an impact within the district, such party may, as a result, subject itself to the personal jurisdiction of the courts of that district—this is known as long-arm jurisdiction.

Proper venue is, as you should by now suspect, a matter of statute. For a long time, the applicable law—set forth in the Federal Rules of Civil Procedure (FRCP) (Title 28 of the United States Code)—was that actions pertaining to patent infringement could be brought only "in the judicial district where the defendant resides, or where the defendant has committed acts of infringement and has a regular and established place of business" (28 U.S.C. §1400(b)). Thus, an infringer could be sued only in those jurisdictions where it had a place of business. Obviously, such a requirement could comprise a serious limitation on a plaintiff's choice of forum.

In 1990, however, following certain changes in the law, it was determined that a defendant corporation could also be sued for patent infringement "in any judicial district in which it is subject to personal jurisdiction at the time the action is commenced" (28 U.S.C. §1391(c)). This meant that a corporation could be sued in a jurisdiction where it had no place of business, if it had committed acts sufficient to subject it to long-arm jurisdiction. Given that many infringing companies commit their nefarious acts on a nationwide basis, this change in the law is indeed liberating to plaintiffs. (*Note:* This does *not* mean that such an infringer may be sued anywhere the plaintiff may choose; other requirements must still be satisfied. Consult an attorney.)

At this point, you are likely asking, "Why read this arcane (euphemism for 'boring') stuff? What difference does it make where suit is brought?" The answer is: It makes a lot of difference.

The first difference is one of convenience. Given a choice of venues, a plaintiff may choose the most convenient one (*convenient* is a euphemism for "least costly"). For example, by choosing a court near its principal place of business, a plaintiff may reduce the travel time and expense of its witnesses. Selection of a court near the offices of the plaintiff's trial counsel obviates the need for a local counsel—a significant cost savings. The plaintiff's selection may prove to increase the defendant's costs, but this, of course, is purely coincidental (right!).

A plaintiff may choose a venue where it expects to receive public (jury) sympathy and support; or it may choose to avoid a venue where the defendant enjoys such popularity.

Finally, although there is now a great deal of similarity—indeed homogeneity—between federal courts, some differences still remain. Different precedents may be followed. Also, backlogs and scheduling practices vary among the various districts. In some districts, it can be reliably predicted that trial will follow the initiation of an action by three or even four years. In other districts (the so-called "rocket dockets"), trial may commence in less than a year. All of these factors must be identified and weighed before a venue is chosen.

## A Jury Is a Good Thing

It has long been believed—often correctly—that juries are unable to comprehend the complex technical questions presented by a patent infringement lawsuit. For that reason, most litigants formerly waived their right to a jury trial, opting instead for a bench trial—a trial in which the judge both applies the law *and* determines the facts to which the law is applied (the function performed by the jury when one is present). Bench trials tend to result in approximately equal numbers of verdicts for the plaintiff/patentee, and the defendant/(alleged) infringer. (The actual historical number is 51% of decisions in favor of the plaintiffs.)

About two decades ago, however, a truly brilliant (but unknown) member of the plaintiffs' bar (the good guys) realized that this lack of understanding could be turned to the plaintiffs' advantage. This is because, by law, an issued patent is presumed to be valid. If, as is virtually always the case, a defendant alleges that the patent(s)-in-suit are invalid, the defendant has the burden of proving the invalidity by "clear and convincing evidence." This burden of proof is considerably more demanding than the ordinary burden in civil (noncriminal) matters—a mere "preponderance of the evidence." Thus, a jury, which is, almost certainly, totally confused by the esoteric technical evidence adduced (lawyerspeak for "introduced") by the learned (lawyerspeak for "expensive") counsel, is unlikely to find that the defense has met this burden. Rather, the jury will find—in effect, by default—that the patent(s)-in-suit is "not invalid." (Just as criminal suspects are not found innocent, but rather "not guilty," so, too, patents are not found "valid," but rather "not invalid.")

Lest the jury overlook this factor, plaintiff's counsel reminds them of it during closing arguments. Moreover, juries (more so than judges) are apt to decide *all* of the issues in favor of the same party. If a jury finds in favor of the plaintiff with respect to the validity of the patent(s)-in-suit, so too is it likely to find that the patent(s) are infringed. The ultimate result is that a jury is considerably more likely than a judge to enter a verdict in favor of the plaintiff (historically, the probability is 68%). The conclusion to be drawn is that, in most cases (lawyers rarely speak in absolute terms—there are too often exceptions to any rule), *a plaintiff should request a jury trial.*

Juries do, nonetheless, present some special problems, most of which derive from the simple fact that juries are composed of normal people.

They become bored. They become irate. Unlike the attorneys and the expert witnesses (and, to a somewhat lesser extent, the judge), they are not receiving substantial compensation for their courtroom duty (as anyone who has served on a jury can attest, jury pay is a pittance).

It is, therefore, extremely important that case presentation in a jury trial be entertaining. Communication skills are paramount (bear this in mind when selecting counsel). Maximum use should be made of visual aids, especially video presentations and computer simulations (if it comes out of a computer, it must be correct!). Do not give the appearance of prolonging the proceeding, and do not appear condescending to the jury. Every opportunity should be seized to present the party in a favorable light—a righteous David locked in mortal combat with a rapacious corporate Goliath.

## Declaratory Judgment Action: The Preemptive Strike

In essence, a declaratory judgment action (in lawyer's jargon, a "DJ action") is a jurisprudential implementation of the old adage, "Do unto others as they would do unto you—only do it first!" It is an opportunity to strike first, rather than waiting for a patentee to file a suit alleging patent infringement. A party, having "standing" (to be discussed in a moment) may file an action in the appropriate ("proper venue") federal court, seeking a judicial declaration that a patent, or patents, are invalid, unenforceable, and/or not infringed by anything the party is doing. Such an action is, in fact, the mirror image of a conventional (euphemism for "boilerplate") patent infringement action. Indeed, the near-universal (knee-jerk) response to a declaratory judgment action is the filing, by the declaratory judgment defendant (the patentee), of a counterclaim alleging (surprise!) patent infringement.

The reader (especially one who has not been paying close attention) may, at this point, ask, "So what? The end result is pretty much the same." The answer is: The end result is not necessarily the same.

First, by filing a declaratory judgment action, the loathsome infringer is able to choose the battlefield. (If this doesn't seem important, reread the section of this chapter entitled "Jurisdiction and Venue.") Second, the disgusting scalawag is able to choose the timing of the action. This may be significant for several reasons. A patentee may, for example, have planned, indeed prepared, to take action against a different infringer (remember that infringement is often industry-wide). These plans and preparations may well be totally upset when the patentee is unexpectedly hauled into a different court to face a different infringer. It is also possible that the patentee is engaged in some activity, such as an IPO, a merger, or an acquisition, that renders litigation especially burdensome at that time.

Finally, many self-proclaimed experts (euphemism for "someone who has actually observed a patent infringement trial") maintain that there is a psychological advantage that accrues to the plaintiff. There may well be something to this theory. Certainly, it is difficult for a patentee to convincingly present a courtroom image of righteous indignation when the only reason he or she is in court is that the (alleged) infringer dragged him there.

"Standing," which is a prerequisite to the bringing of a declaratory judgment action, is, essentially, a requirement that the plaintiff (the pestilential infringer) have an objectively reasonable apprehension of imminent suit by the (righteous, oppressed) patentee. An express charge of infringement by the patentee is not required to create such an apprehension. Rather, the courts look at the totality of the circumstances. Briefly and bluntly put, almost any assertion concerning the scope of a patent will confer standing, whether such assertion is made directly to actual or potential infringers or indirectly, through advertising. The few possible exceptions include the offer of a license without an accompanying charge of infringement, sending copies of one's patents to a competitor (again, without a charge of infringement), and (the authors' personal favorite) lighthearted banter falling short of a threat (the "smile when you say that" exception).

The lesson to be learned is this: Take care when communicating with possible infringers, or an inconvenient declaratory judgment action may result.

# Damages

The court will award to a successful patent infringement plaintiff damages sufficient to place the plaintiff in the position that the plaintiff would have occupied had the infringement not occurred. Just as there are two kinds of infringement (literal infringement and infringement under the doctrine of equivalents), so, too, are there two kinds of damages—lost profits and a reasonable royalty.

Lost profits are, in fact, exactly what they would seem to be—the profits lost by a patentee when an infringer makes sales that, but for the infringement, would have been made by the patentee. The profits in question are incremental profits (i.e., the excess of sale price over variable cost), not net profit, which is gross profit less overhead and other fixed and apportioned costs.

In order to satisfy the "but for" requirement, the patentee must establish that (1) it had the ability or capacity to make the sales it claims to have lost; and (2) there was no noninfringing alternative, such that the subject sales of the defendant were possible only through infringement. It is this second requirement that now may prove to be the greatest stumbling block to a successful patent infringement plaintiff seeking an award of lost profits. Formerly, an infringer was required to show actual

**IN THE REAL WORLD**

# Losing Lost Profits

In *Grain Processing Corp. v. American Maize-Products Co.*, 185 F.3d 1341 (CAFC 1999), the CAFC affirmed a lower court ruling that a patent owner could not recover lost profits if noninfringing substitutes would have been available at the time of infringement.

possession of this noninfringing alternative—an unlikely situation. Clearly, if one actually possessed a substitute for the infringing product or process, there would have been no point in infringing.

Recently, however, the court has greatly relaxed this requirement (see the "Losing Lost Profits" box on this page). Today, an infringer merely needs to establish that the noninfringing alternative was reasonably available. Indeed, it need not have actually been in existence at the time of the infringement, so long as it could have been made available if desired. The effect of this altered requirement is to greatly reduce the probability that a plaintiff will be awarded damages in the form of lost profits.

The damages awarded by the court shall be "in no event less than a reasonable royalty" (35.U.S.C. §284). Clearly, therefore, a reasonable royalty is the minimum amount of damages that may be recovered. Often, it is only a small fraction of the amount that would have been awarded had the lost profits standard been applied. That being said, the question remains, "What constitutes a reasonable royalty?"

In theory, a reasonable royalty is the royalty that would have been agreed upon by a willing licensor and a willing licensee at the time the infringement began. The factors that theoretically would have been considered by the parties are set forth in the Georgia-Pacific case (*Georgia-Pacific Corp. v. United States Plywood Corp.,* 318 F.Supp. 1116 [S.D.N.Y. 1970]). In practice, of course, a reasonable royalty is whatever

**EXHIBIT 8.1**

# Royalty Rates by Industry

| Industry | Avg. Rate | Median Rate | Royalty as % of Profit Rate |
|---|---|---|---|
| **Automotive** | 4.7% | 4.0% | 79.7% |
| **Chemicals** | 4.7% | 3.6% | 25.9% |
| **Computers** | 5.2% | 4.0% | 34.4% |
| **Consumer Goods** | 5.5% | 5.0% | 30.8% |
| **Electronics** | 4.3% | 4.0% | 51.3% |
| **Energy & Environment** | 5.0% | 5.0% | 52.9% |
| **Health Care Products** | 5.8% | 4.8% | 22.4% |
| **Internet** | 11.7% | 7.5% | 492.6% |
| **Machines/ Tools** | 5.2% | 4.5% | 35.8% |
| **Pharma & Biotech** | 7.0% | 5.1% | 17.7% |
| **Semiconductors** | 4.6% | 3.2% | 8.5% |
| **Software** | 10.5% | 6.8% | 22.6% |
| **Telecom** | 5.3% | 4.7% | 35.5% |

Source: Jarosz, John, Carla Mulhern and Robert Vigil. *Industry Royalty Rates and Profitability.* Presented at Licensing Executives Society Annual Meeting, October 31, 2001.

the court decides it to be. The factors that seem to weigh most heavily, however, are the royalty rates in other licenses, if any, granted by the patentee, and that old standby, "the standard rate in the industry" (see Exhibit 8.1).

## But Wait, There's More!

Damages are intended as recompense for the ill effects of the infringement. Yet what are these ill effects? It may be that the patentee suffered a loss of sales, in respect of which it will seek to recover its lost profits. But did it not suffer more? Probably it did; just ask an economist or an accountant (and be prepared to pay for the answer).

Initially, a patentee, by reason of its patent, enjoys a monopoly and may price the patented product or service accordingly. When this monopoly is broken by the despicable acts of an infringer, competition may force the patentee to reduce its price for the patented product. The revenues and, hence, profits lost as a result of this price erosion may be recoverable as damages by the patentee. Although sometimes difficult to establish (to the satisfaction of the court), price erosion can comprise a very significant portion of the total damages resulting from an infringement.

In addition to lost sales of the patented product, the patentee may suffer a loss of sales of associated products or services. Such associated products may be supplies or consumables normally purchased and used in conjunction with the patented product. For example, film purchased in conjunction with patented cameras or razor blades purchased in conjunction with patented razors. The profit lost with the loss of sales of these associated goods, known as *convoyed sales,* is, under appropriate circumstances, recoverable.

Furthermore, along with sales of the patented product, the patentee may have lost sales of spare or replacement parts (which often enjoy a high profit margin) and service or maintenance contracts. Again, the profits lost in this manner may be recoverable as damages. This doctrine of considering the effect of the patent infringement on not only the patentee's sales of the patented product, but also convoyed sales, is known as the *entire market value rule.* This rule may also have application to cases in which damages are awarded in the form of reasonable royalties rather than lost profits.

In cases in which the patentee is in competition with the infringer, but the court nevertheless awards only a reasonable royalty as damages (indicating that a noninfringing alternative was available), the patentee may argue for inclusion of the convoyed sales in the base against which the reasonable royalty is applied; or, alternatively, the patentee may use the existence of such convoyed sales to support an argument for a higher royalty rate (the argument here being that, in view of all the benefits accruing to a licensee, willing parties would have agreed on a higher royalty rate).

# Patent Infringement Litigation—An Overview

In a very general sense, all patent litigations follow a predictable path. However, it must be borne in mind that each case is unique. This individuality arises from a number of factors, including peculiarities of the local rules of the court where the action is being tried, tactical decisions made by the opposing party, and the personal preferences of the trial judge. If patent infringement litigation seems confusing and uncertain, it is!

Patent infringement litigation, like all civil litigation, commences with the filing and service upon the defendant(s) of a summons and complaint. The summons is essentially a notice to the defendant that he/she/it is being sued, identifying the court and the parties and directing the defendant to file an appearance identifying the defendant's attorney. The complaint sets forth, in numbered counts and paragraphs, the specific allegations being leveled against the defendant(s) (i.e., charges of direct infringement, contributory infringement, and inducement to infringe), and ends in a prayer for relief, listing the various forms of relief being sought. Such relief, at a minimum, comprises unspecified monetary damages and an injunction against further infringement; and frequently extends to multiple damages, attorney's fees, costs, interest, and so on. (The list is limited only by the creativity and imagination of the plaintiff's counsel.)

Once served with the summons and complaint, the defendant appears and files an answer, which is a lighthearted denial of all of the material allegations of the complaint, together with a list of affirmative defenses ("I didn't do it, but even if I did—which I deny—it doesn't matter because . . ."). Most defendants will also search high and low for any possible counterclaims, which, if found, are appended to the answer. The plaintiff responds to the answer by filing a reply (this depends on local rules and the defendant's legal budget), including a jocular denial of the allegations of the affirmative defenses. If counterclaims have been made, the plaintiff (now more properly known as the "plaintiff and counterclaim defendant") will jovially deny the allegations thereof as well. At this point, the pleadings are closed and, in most civil litigation (i.e., civil litigation not involving patent infringement), discovery—also known as the discovery process (or the "Chinese water torture")—commences. Patent infringement litigation, however, has been marching to a different drummer since the landmark Supreme Court decision in the *Markman* case.

In *Markman*, for reasons known only to themselves, the Supreme Court justices decided to consider who should "construe" (define, delineate, guess at) the scope of the claims of the patent(s)-in-suit. Being unimpressed by nearly 200 years of consistent American practice, they harkened back to those thrilling days of yore, in olde England, when juries were comprised of ignorant peasants, and contracts, when in dispute, were construed by the more learned (as compared to the peasants) judges. Deciding, by analogy, that modern-day American juries were incapable of comprehending the intricacies of patent claim construction (often true), they decided that the task would best be accomplished if guided by a wise and experienced jurist (often untrue). To this end, they decided that, henceforth, the question of claim construction was one of law, not fact, to be decided by the court (i.e., the trial judge). Thus, we have the genesis of the so-called Markman hearing, which continues to plague us even today.

Although the Supreme Court, in effect, mandated a Markman hearing, it did not specify when in the litigation process this was to occur. Most often, it takes place rather early, following a limited period of discovery directed solely at claim construction issues. In some cases, the

Markman hearing amounts to a "trial before the trial," complete with expert witness testimony and the introduction of excerpts from all manner of printed reference works. Most judges, however, eschew extrinsic evidence, especially the testimony of self-proclaimed experts, and limit the hearing to attorney argument. Indeed, some judges rely solely on written briefs, thus delivering the *Markman* decision without the hearing.

However achieved—either through a full, evidentiary hearing or by divining the entrails—the court ultimately decides the scope and meaning of the patent claims-in-suit. At this point, patent infringement litigation rejoins the regularly scheduled legal programming. Full discovery now commences, with all its breathtaking billing opportunities for the lawyers (discovery costs sometimes run to seven figures). At the close of discovery, the impoverished but unbowed parties appear at trial, to finally be accorded their day (frequently a week or two) in court. Total time elapsed from the filing of the complaint to entry of a verdict: at least nine months, most often about two to three years. It is not uncommon, however, for a case to drag on for four years or more (for further reading, see the case of *Jarndyce v. Jarndyce* described in the novel *Bleak House* by Charles Dickens).

## Popular Misconceptions— The Cloakroom Defenses

A charge of patent infringement often elicits one of two indignant responses: (1) "I'm not infringing your patent because I invented the accused product/service myself" or (2) "I'm not responsible because I purchased the product in question from XYZ Company—talk to them" (invariably, XYZ Company is an offshore entity, well beyond the patent holder's reach). These responses are similar to the little placards posted in restaurant cloakrooms that say "Not responsible for lost or stolen property"—they are effective only if one is gullible enough to believe them.

Unlike copyrights and trade secrets, patents protect against independent recreation—"reinventing the wheel." (This, in part, justifies the greater cost of patents.) Thus, so long as the patent in question is valid (the accused did not make the invention before the patentee did), the subsequent independent invention is not a legal defense. (*Note:* Many are those who claim prior invention, few are those who can prove it. Go ahead and sue the sucker.)

As the reader will (should) remember from Chapter 1, a patent bars the unauthorized practice of the patented invention—making, using, selling, or offering it for sale. It matters not that the seller of a product bought it from another. Everyone in the chain of distribution is equally liable for any infringement. As a practical matter, the (supposedly innocent) seller probably has (or certainly should have) an indemnification agreement with his or her supplier. Indeed, under the Uniform Commercial Code (UCC), the seller impliedly warrants that noncustom goods are free of patent infringement. So again, go ahead and sue the sucker. Let *them* chase the miserable, misbegotten supplier to recover any damages awarded to you.

A slightly less common, but still popular, response (also invariably delivered with great indignation), is "I'm not infringing; I, myself, have a patent on this product." (Usually, however, the grammar isn't this good.) Even if it is true, this will avail the speaker naught. Remember the red fire engine. A patent is a negative right (some things bear repetition). It does not convey the affirmative right to make the patented product. Go ahead and sue the sucker.

## Time Can Mean So Much— Laches and Estoppel

Although not unique to patent litigation cases, two often-encountered defenses are laches and estoppel (some writers mention laches and estoppel as a single defense—this is both incorrect and intellectually sloppy).

*Laches* is the unexcused failure to take action in a timely manner (in lay terms, sitting on your hands). Having once discovered an infringement, a patentee must take action (file suit) with reasonable promptness. If the patentee fails to so act, and the delay causes material prejudice to the (alleged) infringer, the patentee may be barred from recovery of any damages for past acts of infringement—those occurring prior to the filing of the suit. The patentee may, nonetheless, obtain an injunction barring further infringement of the patent(s)-in-suit.

"Prejudice to the (alleged) infringer" refers to a handicap in presenting a defense. A defendant may allege, for example, that critical documents have been discarded as no longer needed, or that key witnesses are no longer available, or that their memories have dimmed (such dimming often proves to be surprisingly selective). Some cases hold that additional or continued investment in specialized plant and equipment or the expansion of the allegedly infringing business, by the defendant, constitutes prejudice. The length of delay is measured from the time the infringement was discovered, or reasonably should have been discovered. A patentee cannot, like Admiral Nelson, turn a blind eye to such evidence of infringement as would prompt further investigation by a reasonable patentee (so-called inquiry notice). Finally, a delay of six years is presumed to be unreasonable (well, duh!)—and creates a "rebuttable presumption" of laches. This has the effect of shifting the burden of proof from the defendant (who otherwise must prove prejudice) to the plaintiff (who must now prove some legally cognizable excuse for the delay).

*Estoppel,* or more properly equitable estoppel, is closely related to laches. Whereas laches involves a mere failure to act, equitable estoppel requires some affirmative act by the patentee that leads an accused infringer to believe that it will remain unmolested (in lay terms, barking, but then failing promptly to bite). The accused infringer must reasonably rely on this act to its detriment. (*Detriment* is largely synonymous with *prejudice* in the context of laches.) Although mere silence does not give rise to equitable estoppel, extended inaction after issuing a notice of infringement may well do so. Equitable estoppel not only bars recovery for past acts of infringement, it renders the patent completely unenforceable with respect to that defendant. The lesson to be learned: Don't bluff. Never accuse others of infringement, nor threaten suit, unless prepared to take legal action.

## Litigation Risk Analysis

Litigation in general, and particularly patent infringement litigation, involves an untold number of decisions: settlement decisions, pretrial discovery decisions, trial strategy decisions, and appeal decisions. Lawyers and business executives are constantly striving to make the right decisions. The process of making these decisions is rendered more difficult by the complexity of the problems being addressed and the uncertainties associated with their various constituent factors. The decision-making process may be facilitated, however, through the use of litigation risk analysis.

Litigation is fraught with uncertainty, which is a condition or a state inherent in situations offering more than one possible outcome. Uncertainty also arises from the inherently probabilistic nature of some of the events affecting the ultimate outcome, as well as from the imperfect information available about certain facts and the concomitant need to make assumptions. Risk is the likelihood that the actual outcome will be unfavorable or undesired. Complexity results from uncertainty piled atop uncertainty. From a business decision-making point of view, litigation management is to a large degree a risk management problem.

Risk is most often difficult to precisely measure or assess. Commonly, it is described with generalities such as "a good chance," "probably," "in all likelihood," or (only slightly better) "more likely than not." Such terms are vague and uncertain, conveying different meaning to different people. More importantly, they cannot be combined to describe the risk presented by a situation involving more than one uncertainty. Such methods of description are obviously unsatisfactory.

Clearly, there is a need to rationalize complex problems, that is, to identify the constituent uncertainties (at least the most significant ones) of the problem and the relations therebetween, to assess the risks associated with these uncertainties and present them in a precise and mathematically sound manner, and to combine these constituent risks so as to determine the risk presented by the entire problem. Litigation risk analysis, which is both a disciplined approach to the analysis of problems involving uncertainty and a systematic method of dealing with complexity, meets this need. Properly applied, it will lead to the identification of the best decision (which, as we will see, is not always the right decision). In addition, it will provide a basis for clear, precise communications.

## Identification of Uncertainties and Drawing the Decision Tree

The first step in litigation risk analysis, indeed in any risk analysis, is to identify and organize all (or at least the significant) uncertainties that comprise a problem. These uncertainties are then schematically arranged in consecutive order, starting with the present and progressing into the future, to produce a flowchart encompassing all of the uncertainties and all of the possible outcomes of the problem. The flowchart is then converted or reformatted as a decision tree. (Some practitioners prefer to omit the flowchart and commence organization and representation of a problem as a decision tree.) Each point of uncertainty causes the tree to branch, with one new branch being created for each possible outcome of the uncertain event. Each possible outcome of the problem is found at the tip of at least one branch. The process of preparing a flowchart and/or a decision tree can best be explained and understood with reference to the following example.

## Example

The client company (the "Client") is one of a small number of firms in the business of producing a mineral product that is first fused in a kiln and then ground. An executive of the client company (the "Executive") quit his job and immediately thereafter invented and subsequently patented an improved kiln. The client company claims ownership of this patent, but has taken no action with respect thereto.

Utilizing the invention, the Executive started a business that competes with the Client. The Client, wishing to upgrade its technology, retained a consultant (the "Consultant") to design improvements to its own kilns. The Client chose not to disclose the patent to the Consultant, who remained unaware of its existence. Based on the Consultant's design, the Client built new kilns, which bear a marked resemblance to those described and claimed in the patent. The Client also improved its grinding procedures. The Client's various changes have caused a substantial improvement in the quality of its product, allowing it to dominate the market.

With his market share and price being steadily eroded, the Executive brought a lawsuit against the Client for patent infringement. The Executive claims that the alleged infringement is willful and seeks lost profits and treble damages.

The Client has responded to the suit by denying infringement and asserting that the patent is invalid. The Client further asserts its ownership of the patent, alleging that the Executive made the invention while in the Client's employ. Obtaining a stay of proceedings in the infringement action, the Client has petitioned for reexamination of the patent on the basis of prior art not considered during examination of the original patent application. This reexamination resulted in a final rejection of all of the claims-in-suit. An appeal of this rejection to the Patent Office Board of Appeals is now pending.

The Client has calculated that, if found guilty of patent infringement, a reasonable royalty for use of the patented kiln would be $500,000, while the Executive's lost profits would amount to $10 million. It is believed that the choice of the appropriate measure of damages will depend on a finding as to whether the improvement in quality of the Client's product was the result of the change in the Client's kiln design (i.e., whether the output of the accused kiln is unique).

Finally, it is anticipated that in-house staff will handle all proceedings in this matter and, hence, no legal fees will be incurred.

The Client has requested a decision as to the settlement value of this case. As a first step in reaching such a decision, a model or flowchart of the litigation, as shown in Exhibit 8.2, would be prepared. The top or first three boxes are included merely to place the problem in its historical context. As past events, they could have been omitted.

Presented in Exhibit 8.3 is the same problem analysis in the form of a decision tree.

**IN THE REAL WORLD**

## The Odds Against Going to Trial

Seventy-six percent of patent suits settle, but generally not until each side incurs roughly $1 million in legal fees. Only about 4% of patent infringement lawsuits proceed through trial.

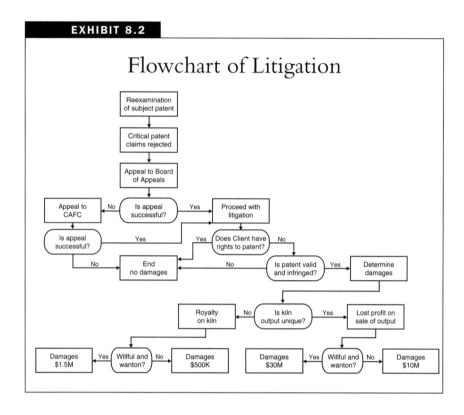

EXHIBIT 8.2

The decision tree lists all of the identified uncertainties of the present problem and graphically illustrates the relations between them. All of the possible outcomes are listed in the column to the right of the tree. As yet, however, there has been no consideration of the risks engendered by these uncertainties. We cannot, therefore, determine the likelihood of any of these outcomes actually occurring.

## Assessing the Risks

Having identified all of the uncertainties and, therefore, being aware of what *can* happen, we must now assess the risks associated therewith; which is to say we must determine the *likelihood* or probability of each of the possible outcomes actually occurring.

# Decision Tree Analysis of Litigation

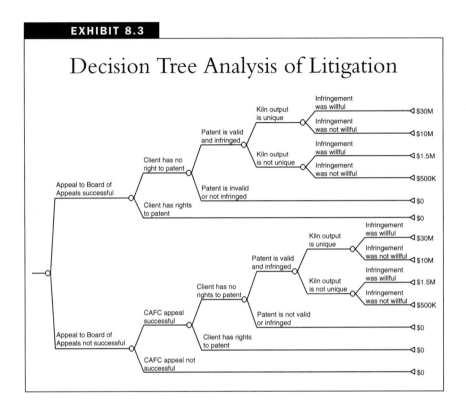

In general, attorneys are loath to assign probabilities to risks. This may be due to a perceived inability to make an accurate assessment or (more likely) a fear that the assessment may prove inaccurate and "come back to haunt." (One attorney claimed that his malpractice insurance carrier would not permit him to offer percentage assessments of risk.) However difficult it may prove to be, there is, unfortunately, no alternative to obtaining risk assessments from the people most intimately involved and knowledgeable about the problem. Soliciting assessments from several individuals and assuring them that only the resulting average will be utilized can sometimes overcome this reluctance. (This approach has been compared to recruiting members for a firing squad by assuring them that one of them will have a blank cartridge in his rifle.)

A better approach (although much more cumbersome and time consuming) is the so-called Delphi Oracle, which involves soliciting opinions (in this case, risk assessments) from a number of individuals, who are most commonly kept separated and anonymous to prevent status, authority, or other intimidating influences from prejudicing their views. After all of the participants have submitted an assessment, those who have submitted the most extreme opinions (in our case, the highest and lowest risk assessments) are informed of the opinions of the others and offered an opportunity to reconsider (euphemism for "change") their own opinions. If they decline this opportunity, they are required to state their reasons for maintaining their extreme position. These reasons are then conveyed to the other participants who are then offered the opportunity to reconsider *their* opinions. If they decline to alter their opinions, they must respond to the reasons provided by the extremists. Any reasons so provided are then conveyed to the extremists, who are once again presented with the choice of revising (another euphemism for "changing") their opinion or defending it. Generally, after two or three such iterations, something approaching consensus is reached.

Continuing with this example, the risks therein were assessed as shown in Exhibit 8.4.

Having obtained these risk assessments, we are now ready to complete our example litigation risk analysis.

## Putting It All Together

Once the risks inherent in a problem have been assessed, they are entered on the previously prepared decision tree. In Exhibit 8.5, the risk assessments, in the form of probabilities, have been entered on the decision tree.

The probability that a given outcome will actually occur may now be calculated. It is the mathematical combination of each of the risks

EXHIBIT 8.4

# Risk Assessment

| | |
|---|---|
| Probability that the Patent Office Board of Appeals will reverse the Patent Examiner's rejection of the critical reexamined claims | 30% |
| Probability that the CAFC would reverse a decision of the Board of Appeals affirming the claims rejection | 30% |
| Probability that the Client is found, by the Court, to have rights to the patent in suit | 10% |
| Probability that the reexamined patent is found by the Court to be both valid and infringed | 80% |
| Probability that the Court determines that the patented kiln caused the increase in quality of the Client's product | 80% |
| Probability that, if found guilty of infringement, the Court will determine the infringement to have been willful and wanton | 50% |

encountered along the path between that outcome and the start point. (Risks are combined by multiplying them together.) The probability of occurrence of each of the possible outcomes is listed in Exhibit 8.6. The sum of the probabilities of occurrence of each of the possible outcomes is 1.0 (or 100%), meaning that (if our model is accurate) one of these outcomes must occur. (If this total is other than 1.0, or 100%, an arithmetic error was made somewhere.) The third column in Exhibit 8.6, entitled Expected Value, lists the product of each possible outcome multiplied by the likelihood or probability that it will actually occur. The sum of the expected values is the expected value of all possible outcomes and, hence, the probabilistic outcome of the problem. In our example, it is the effective value of the case—$2.46 million—that represents the effective potential liability or "exposure" to the Client.

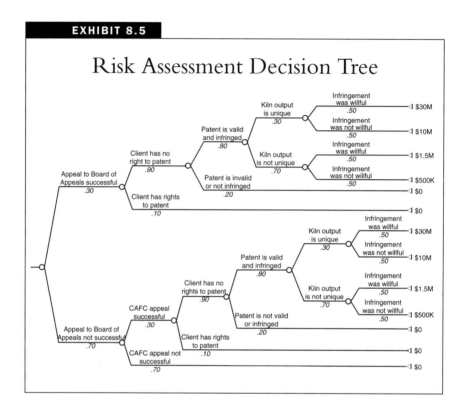

EXHIBIT 8.5

# Risk Assessment Decision Tree

Once the analysis is complete, it should be subjected to a sanity test (i.e., is the result so outrageous as to suggest that it is likely to be erroneous?). (*Hint:* If the result seems unreasonable, but the sum of the possible outcomes is 1.0, the error is likely in the model; either the flowchart is wrong or an error was made in converting it into a decision tree.)

Once reasonably confident that the risk analysis is sane, it may be enlightening to determine the sensitivity of the model or the criticality of the various uncertainties that comprise the problem. This is done by altering the assessment of the risk associated with the uncertainty and observing the impact on the sum of the expected values (a procedure known as *sensitivity analysis*). Such sensitivity analysis may disclose the importance of a seemingly minor issue or, conversely, may reveal that a supposedly key issue is actually of relatively little significance.

EXHIBIT 8.6

# Probability Table

| Possible Outcome ($ Million) | Probability | Expected Value ($ Million) |
|---|---|---|
| $ 30.0 | 3.24% | $ .97 |
| $ 10.0 | 3.24% | $ .32 |
| $ 1.5 | 7.56% | $ .11 |
| $ 0.5 | 7.56% | $ .04 |
| $ 0 | 5.40% | $ 0 |
| $ 0 | 3.00% | $ 0 |
| $ 30.0 | 2.27% | $ .68 |
| $ 10.0 | 2.27% | $ .23 |
| $ 1.5 | 5.29% | $ .08 |
| $ 0.5 | 5.29% | $ .03 |
| $ 0 | 3.78% | $ 0 |
| $ 0 | 2.10% | $ 0 |
| $ 0 | 49.0% | $ 0 |
| $ 84 | 100% | $ 2.46 |

Finally, the analysis should be examined to determine whether it contradicts any conventional wisdom or other widely accepted views. For instance, in our example, despite the rather pessimistic views regarding the Executive's chances of securing allowance of the critical patent claims, we learn that, in fact, he has a 51% probability of success. This is comprised of a 30% probability that the Board of Appeals will reverse the patent examiner, and a 21% probability (.70 × .30 = .21) that an appeal will be taken to the CAFC and decided in favor of the Executive. It is "more likely than not," barring settlement, that the Client will have to face him at trial.

## Tips and Techniques

When making decisions based on a decision tree risk analysis, it must always be borne in mind that, in real life, unlikely outcomes do sometimes occur. Indeed, our analysis calculates the finite probability that such out-comes will occur. If such an outcome would have a serious (or even cat-astrophic) effect, it cannot be safely ignored.

The likelihood of being unpleasantly surprised by such a probabilis-tically unexpected outcome can be reduced if the decision tree is updat-ed as each of the included future events becomes an historic event. After the time for an event to occur has passed, its probability of occurrence is either 100% (it did occur) or 0% (it did not occur), and the previous-ly estimated probability for the event should be replaced with the his-torically determined one.

**IN THE REAL WORLD**

# The Real Deal

The foregoing example was drawn from a real case managed by one of the authors. As the case unfolded

❶ The Board of Appeals affirmed the patent examiner's rejection of the critical reexamined claims.

❷ The CAFC reversed the Board of Appeals.

❸ The court found that the Client did not have any rights to the patent-in-suit.

❹ The court found the reexamined patent to be valid and infringed.

❺ The court found the patented kiln caused the increase in quali-ty of the Client's product, awarding damages on a "lost profits" basis.

❻ The court found the infringement to have been willful and wan-ton, and awarded treble damages.

The net result of the case (from the Client's view) was an adverse judgment in excess of $30 million. The expected probability of this event was only 2.27%, yet it did occur!

## Dealing with Complexity and Moving into the Modern Age

As mentioned at the beginning of this chapter, patent infringement litigation presents an exceedingly large number of risks, some of which are common to all litigation, while others are peculiar to patent matters. The patent-specific issues relate to the questions of patent validity, patent enforceability, and patent infringement, and to damages calculation. These questions, and some of the subissues of which they are comprised, are set forth in the following list.

How likely is it that the patent will be found to be

*Invalid* due to

- Prior art (anticipation, obviousness)

- Lack of enablement

- Failure to disclose the best mode

*Unenforceable* due to

- Inequitable conduct

- Laches

- Estoppel

- Patent misuse

**IN THE REAL WORLD**

## More Patent Litigation Odds

Only 1.1% of all patents are ever litigated. About 67% of patents litigated through trial remain valid, and only 11–12% of patents are held unenforceable. Sixty-six percent of patents are found infringed at trial.

*Not infringed* as to

- Claim 1

- Claim 2

- Claim X

Infringement analysis should preferably be performed for each claim of the asserted patents (at the very least, the independent claims). Once this analysis is completed, further questions may be asked (see Exhibit 8.7).

In addition to the foregoing, it is to be considered that the level of complexity of patent infringement litigation has been vastly increased by the requirement of a so-called Markman hearing which, in effect, adds another layer of litigation—a trial before the trial—to the resolution of a patent infringement case.

By this time, the keen observer will have noted that each uncertainty added to a decision tree results in a substantial increase in the number of tree branches. Indeed, a single uncertainty (with only two possible outcomes) added at the roots of the tree may double the number of branches in the completed tree. It will be appreciated, therefore, that as an analysis of a problem becomes more detailed, the resultant decision tree spreads even further, becoming cumbersome, if not impossible, to

**EXHIBIT 8.7**

## Infringement Analysis Questions

| 1 | What is the probability that a motion seeking a preliminary injuction will be granted? |
|---|---|
| 2 | What is the probability that a motion for summary judgment on (a) invalidity, (b) unenforceability, (c) noninfringement, or (d) infringement will be granted? |
| 3 | After a decision for the plaintiff, will the damages be assessed based on lost profits or reasonable royalties? |
| 4 | Will infringement be found to have been wanton (i.e., will multiple damages be awarded)? |
| 5 | Will the case be deemed exceptional (i.e., will attorney's fees be awarded)? |

manually handle. Combining closely related or intertwined uncertainties may sometimes ameliorate this problem. Thus, in our example, patent validity and infringement were combined. In real life, this analysis would be an oversimplification. However, combining—as a single uncertainty —the validity of all claims in a patent (based on the notion that all claims stand or fall together), or even so considering the validity of several patents within a portfolio of patents, may be a reasonable simplification. Indeed, if an assessment of the risk of patent validity is impossible (or inconvenient) to obtain, historical data may be substituted. For example, juries have historically found patents not valid 67% of the time, and judges, in bench trials, have found them not valid 57% of the time.

It should also be noted that, despite the considerable effort required, the risk assessments in the example given were developed as a single number. Obviously, a range of probabilities, rather than a single number, is more likely to be correct and less troublesome to obtain. Although mathematical formulae exist allowing for the use of ranges rather than discrete assessments of risk, such approaches are exceedingly complex and unsuitable for use by the practitioner. Fortunately, this problem is neatly solved by what is known as Monte Carlo simulation.

Simply stated, Monte Carlo simulation utilizes random numbers to determine the actual outcome of the various uncertainties composing a problem. Each complete simulation represents one possible outcome of the problem. The simulation is repeated many times to create a statistical analysis of all possible outcomes of a problem. Thus, unlike the simple analysis of our example (which produced a single number representing the *expected value* of all possible outcomes), Monte Carlo simulation yields a *distribution* of all possible outcomes with their corresponding probability of occurrence. Rather than purporting to tell *what* will happen, Monte Carlo simulation specifies *how likely* any possible outcome actually is. Such a simulation also offers a fine opportunity to perform a sensitivity analysis.

## TIPS & TECHNIQUES

As might be expected, various computer software packages are available that both assist in the creation of decision trees and facilitate the simple or Monte Carlo analysis thereof. For decision tree analysis, the authors highly recommend the Data 3.5 software from TreeAge Software, Inc., which was used for this chapter. This software is available with a handy user guide from Litigation Risk Analysis, Inc.

## Choosing and Managing Your Counsel

One cannot fight a war without an army. Similarly, one cannot litigate a patent without a squad of lawyers. Selecting a law firm is a critical, but not unduly complex, task. Only three basic factors must be considered: quality, flexibility, and price.

### "A Few Good Men" (Women)

There is an ancient Chinese proverb that holds, "Gold will not always buy you good soldiers, but good soldiers will always bring you gold." Despite this long-standing recognition of the primacy of quality over price, many prospective plaintiffs focus on price when selecting a law firm to litigate their patent(s). *Do not do this.* Pay what is necessary to retain the best people. If one wins, few will worry about the cost. If one loses, the saving of a few dollars offers little consolation.

Having decided to hire the best counsel, the question remains how to identify them. Often, people look to recent, newsworthy trials, seeking to hire the firm that represented the prevailing party. While this approach has some basis in logic, it is good to remember that even a clock that has stopped is right twice a day. Therefore, inquire also about the cases that the firm has lost.

For all of its shortcomings, the newspaper technique, along with recommendations from colleagues, may be the best means of assembling a list of candidate firms. To select a firm from amongst these candidates, they must be interviewed and critically analyzed.

Interviewing can best be accomplished by first preparing a brief (one-page) synopsis of the case and forwarding it to each of the candidate firms, having first verified that they have no conflicts that would prevent them from accepting the matter and that they are also willing to accept the synopsis and discuss it. Some firms may be unwilling to accept the proffered synopsis, either because of a preexisting conflict or because they hope to be retained by the opposing party. Thus, the identification of such firms may be a useful bit of intelligence. Further, those firms that review the synopsis may be thereby barred from later representing the opposing party. Thus, even an unsuccessful interview is not without its benefit.

Law firms do not litigate cases—lawyers do. When interviewing a law firm, insist on speaking with the lawyers who will actually handle the case. Do not be satisfied with platitudes from the firm's managing partner whose only involvement with the matter, after a retainer agreement has been signed, is to review and increase (more on this later) the billings in the matter. When speaking to the attorney who would be chiefly responsible for the matter, ask what strengths and weaknesses are perceived in the case, and what strategy is planned. Obviously, such preliminary opinions and plans are subject to revision as further information is acquired. Nevertheless, the interviewee attorney should be familiar with the information provided, should have identified the key issues presented by the case, and should be able to propose a comprehensive and realistic case strategy.

Occasionally, an interviewee will have researched the matter prior to the interview. Such efforts show initiative or at least a strong desire to secure a new client. If such research was done, consider it carefully. Did it focus on relevant matters? Was it productive (i.e., did it increase the likelihood of success)? Not all research is relevant or productive (although it is all expensive). An attorney who lacks focus at an interview will almost certainly lack focus throughout the case.

No (sane, responsible) attorney will undertake to litigate a patent infringement case of any significance alone. Most commonly, the lead attorney will be a partner or senior associate of the firm. A colleague, generally a midlevel associate, will assist the lead attorney. Inquire about this assistant, and, if possible, include the assistant in the interview. How long have the assistant and lead counsel worked together? Long association indicates that the lead counsel prefers to work with this associate, which, in turn, suggests a measure of respect for the associate's abilities.

## Many Are the Soldiers, Few Are the Fighters

Many attorneys hold themselves out as litigators. Do not confuse *litigators* with *trial attorneys*. The bulk of the work in litigation takes place outside of the courtroom—discovery (interrogatories, requests for production, document review, and depositions) comprises the vast majority of any litigation effort, especially in intellectual property litigation. Legal issues must be resolved and briefs must be drafted. Arguing of motions and the trial itself comprise a very small, but crucial, fraction of the litigation effort. Many litigators spend virtually their entire careers on such preparatory matters and have little or no experience in presenting a case to a trier of fact—either a jury or a judge. Effective presentation calls for a unique set of skills: the ability to simplify without appearing condescending, the ability to think rapidly under pressure, the ability to capture and hold the attention of the judge and the jury, and stage presence (a trial is, after all, theater). These are the peculiar skills of the trial attorney, a much less numerous breed than the litigator. Meet the individual(s) who will actually present the case. Are they compelling? If they make their client drowsy, imagine what they will do to a jury (which probably doesn't want to be in the courtroom in the first place). Nothing is more disheartening than to see a good, well-prepared case lost through ineffective presentation at trial. Be certain that the litigation team includes a first-class trial attorney.

## The Willow, Not the Oak

Patent infringement litigation is a lengthy process. It is, under the best of circumstances, exhausting and exasperating. Conflict with one's counsel can make it infinitely worse. Everything possible should be done to ensure that cordial working relations will be maintained. Such relations require compatible personalities and a reasonable degree of flexibility on the part of counsel.

The requisite flexibility will manifest itself in a number of ways. First, the chosen counsel must share the client's views and attitudes concerning the case to be litigated. This does not mean that the search is for a sycophant—to the contrary, counsel is most effective when espousing beliefs he shares; and an attorney who will meekly adopt the views of the client will often, just as meekly, surrender critical issues to opposing counsel. Nevertheless, if one doesn't agree with counsel before the firing begins, the disagreements will only grow more acrimonious when the bullets begin to fly. (*Note:* If, after extensive searching, no competent counsel can be found with whom one agrees, one should consider the possibility that one has an unreasonable view of the matter or a poor case.)

Second, counsel should be willing to work not only *for* the client, but also *with* the client. However diligent and expert the counsel, it is likely that the client will have better knowledge of all of the relevant facts and circumstances of the case. Moreover, as a case proceeds, lawyers tend to narrow their focus. It is incumbent on the client to maintain a more global perspective, maintaining awareness of changing conditions in the industry and in the circumstances of the parties. Litigation should serve the client's needs, not drive them. An alert and participatory client can assure that tactics, and even strategy, are promptly and appropriately modified to meet changing circumstances. This requires that the client remain informed of all matters in the case and that the attorney is willing and able to accept changes to the battle plan during the heat of battle.

Virtually all counsel will promise to keep the client informed as to the developments in the case. Many, but not all of them, truly mean it. However, such promises mean different things to different people. Counsel should provide information in such a way that there is time to act on it. Information received "after the fact" (i.e., copies of documents already filed) are of merely historical value. Ideally, preliminary drafts, or outlines, of briefs and motions should be provided, such that the client can effectively contribute to finalization of the document with minimal, if any, disruption. Similarly, plans and tactics for depositions should be discussed *before* the depositions are taken.

There are three basic approaches to attorney compensation (being professionals, attorneys are "compensated," not "paid" for their services): fixed fees, time-based billing, and contingency fees. However, various combinations of these three approaches exist.

Fixed fees are best suited to matters where the amount of work to be done is highly predictable; for this reason, they are virtually never encountered in patent infringement litigation.

Time-based billing, also known as hourly billing, is the approach most favored by patent litigators and, hence, is the approach most commonly utilized. Unlike contingency fees, hourly billing involves no risk to the law firm that it will not be paid for its services. At the same time, it allows the client to pay for only those services actually provided. Assuming that the client has the cash available to pay the (generally) monthly invoices from the law firm, time-based billing is probably the preferred compensation scheme for the client as well.

Time-based billing is, however, not without its drawbacks. Foremost among those drawbacks is the lack of incentive to work efficiently or otherwise minimize costs. If left unchecked, overstaffing and the use of senior-level people to do junior-level work may occur. These problems are most prevalent in larger firms. Indeed, after analyzing much empirical data, the following law of nature (modestly known as Lerner's Law) has been discovered:

- There is little relationship between price and quality.
- There is little relationship between the size of a law firm and quality.
- There is a significant relationship between the size of a law firm and the prices it will charge.

It is not to be concluded that large law firms are evil or dishonest; but size, beyond a certain point, imposes diseconomies of scale, as marketing and management become ever more important to the life of the firm (and the success of its members). In general, if counsel is to be retained on a time-based billing approach, it is best to retain a firm that is just large enough to handle the matter in question.

## They Also Bill Who Only Stand and Wait

Another cost-containment measure is to insist on detailed bills specifying the tasks performed by each timekeeper, each day, and the amount of time devoted thereto—so-called task-based billing. This billing format is available from all law firms. If one insists on it, they will comply. The analysis of task-based bills can provide much useful information (there are firms, known as law-audit firms, that specialize in performing such analyses). In particular, task-based billing has the beneficial effect of restraining the tendency of law firms to overstaff (a practice formerly known as overmanning) a matter; for example, sending three attorneys to a deposition when only two would suffice. Also, by identifying the various timekeepers who are billing time to a matter, task-based billing highlights the introduction of new players to the team. This is important because new players must be brought up to speed—briefed on the facts and the status of the case, a process that is time consuming (both the briefer and the briefee are billing their time) and, hence, costly. The obvious goal is to involve the fewest possible people in the case. A client should be careful not to let lawyers use his or her case as a convenient account to which they can bill otherwise unbillable time (this practice should be familiar to anyone who has worked for a government contractor), nor allow the firm to use his or her case as a training vehicle for interns and new associates. Let them train their employees at someone else's expense. Moreover, law firms that know that they are being monitored simply perform more efficiently.

Check on a firm's policy with respect to disbursements. Some firms take a surprisingly narrow view of what is covered by their hourly fees —virtually everything is a disbursement. One firm, in the authors' experience, charged a fee for the use of the firm's own library. Another firm (more aggressive than creative) simply tacked on a "Misc. fee." A surprising number of firms will mark up their disbursements, adding a profit margin. Sometimes this is disguised as an accounting fee or administrative fee. Such a markup is unethical if it is not disclosed to the client, and tacky when it is. Some firms will add an overtime charge to a client's bill, reflecting additional compensation paid to support staff who may have worked late. Such changes may be acceptable when the overtime was necessitated by the demands of the case. They are clearly not acceptable when they result from poor scheduling or understaffing by the firm.

Read legal bills carefully, and do not hesitate to object to charges that may be improper or staffing practices that may be considered undesirable. Do this promptly (if 'twere done, 'twere best done quickly), before the amounts in dispute grow.

Finally, pay legal bills promptly. The law firm is not a banker and has not agreed to finance the litigation. A client that pays on time is in a much better position to win concessions from its law firm.

## Sharing the Risks—And the Rewards

Contingency fees involve an agreement between the client and the law firm that the latter will be compensated solely out of the proceeds of the case. Some law firms will also advance the funds needed to litigate the case—the costs of litigation (e.g., filing and service fees, fees for expert witnesses and court reporters, and travel expenses); others will not. In either event, it is readily apparent that the law firm has accepted the risk that it will not be paid, or that it will not be paid in full. If the law firm has advanced the costs of litigation, it runs the further risk of losing the funds it has advanced. To compensate for this risk, and also simply because they have the economic power to do so, law firms that undertake cases on a contingency basis typically demand a percentage of the projected recovery, which would yield a fee three to four times the fee that would have been accrued on a time-based fee basis. Thus, it should be clear that the contingency fee arrangement is the most costly to the client and should be utilized only out of necessity. It may (rarely) occur that a law firm will undertake a patent infringement case on a contingency basis.

It is "common knowledge" that lawyers, undertaking a case on such a basis, take a third of any recovery. This is a gross oversimplification. Like most things in life, lawyers' contingency fees are subject to negotiation. Even in a contingency arrangement, there should be a correlation between the effort expended and the reward reaped. Few patent infringement suits actually proceed through trial (only about 4%); most are settled. Settlement can occur at any point in the proceedings (although, most commonly, after the Markman hearing). It is this fact that provides the basis for negotiation. Often, the firm will agree to a graduated scale of recovery, with the rate tied to the "stage" at which the matter is concluded.

As might well be suspected, there are numerous possible combinations of the three basic fee approaches. Often, such blended arrangements include a cap on any contingency fee, often coupled with a guaranteed minimum. The "best" arrangement is the one that best serves the needs of the parties. That being said, a fee arrangement preferred by the authors involves an equal mixture of time-based billing and contingency fee. The client pays the costs of litigation and one half of the conventional time-based fee, and agrees to pay one half of the conventional contingency fee. Since most law firms have an overhead rate of 40% to 50%, such an arrangement eliminates their risk in the matter—at worst, they will break even. At the same time, the sizeable contingency provides motivation to succeed. If several firms reject such an arrangement or decline to take a case on a conventional contingency fee basis, it might be considered that they are, cumulatively, saying something about the perceived merits of the case (or lack of same).

## Strategies and Tactics of Enforcement

Tactics is the plan for fighting a battle. Strategy is the plan for winning the war (i.e., reaching the specified objective).

Successful patent enforcement, like a successful military operation, often hinges on the possession of intelligence (i.e., knowledge of the enemy). In business, intelligence gathering is called market research and competitive analysis. Gather as much intelligence as possible before embarking on a campaign of patent enforcement. Continue intelligence-gathering activities until the campaign has ended.

Note that patent enforcement is described in terms of a campaign. Patent infringement is, most often, not confined to a single offender. Frequently, it spreads across an industry. If an infringer is identified, investigate its competitors. It is likely that at least some of them are infringing as well. If such is the case, a program of patent enforcement becomes a campaign against an industry.

When the patent owner identifies one or more infringers, it is considered only sporting for him or her to write to such infringers to offer them a license. Further, there is always the chance, however remote, that the recipient of such a letter will respond favorably (i.e., they will take a license). Stranger things have happened. In any event, there is little to lose, so long as the letter does not provide the recipient with standing to bring a declaratory judgment action. Review all such letters carefully, with counsel, before mailing them.

## Choosing a Defendant

When gentle persuasion proves unsuccessful, it is time to take up the cudgel. Having identified multiple infringers, the first question that must be addressed is which infringer(s) to sue first. The recommendation is often made, more often by well-intentioned laypersons (here a euphemism for "idiots;" known to lawyers as "officious intermeddlers") than by experienced attorneys, to first tackle the biggest and strongest infringer. The theory here is that, after successfully defeating such an infringer, all others will fall into line, taking licenses without further fuss. *Do not listen to such people.* Such advice is tantamount to butting one's head against a wall in preference to opening a door and walking through. Choose the weakest opponent, not the strongest one; choose the one most likely to settle, not the one most likely (and able) to resist.

While there is invariably great reluctance on the part of most business executives to be the first to take a license under a patent, or patent portfolio, there is much less reluctance to be the second. As the number of licensees grows, each successive license becomes easier to conclude. This being so, there is good reason to leave the most intransigent offenders to be dealt with last. Also, as the number of licensees grows, the cost of the licenses increases. Thus, the most difficult and recalcitrant infringers, dealt with last, generally pay the most—proving that there is some justice in the world.

Having decided to first harvest the low-hanging fruit, the question devolves to one of identification: Which infringers are least likely to mount an aggressive defense? This is an area where intelligence proves its worth. Corporations, like natural persons, have personalities—some are aggressive gamblers, others are risk averse. Much can be learned from studying an infringer's past history. Does it litigate often? When it does litigate, does it settle early or fight to the bitter end? Publicly traded firms, managed by professional managers, tend to be more conservative than privately held concerns. Corporate managers fear shareholder reaction to a costly defeat. Small firms, in which the founder is the president and owns all, or most of the equity, should be approached with particular care. Such leaders are often strongly opinionated and answerable to no one. Suing one of these companies is often akin to attacking a tar baby; and even when victory is achieved, the costs may exceed the amount recovered.

Another factor to be considered when selecting a first target is the possibility of so-called pendant claims—claims, other than patent infringement, that arise out of the same activity of the defendant. For example, there may also be claims for trademark or copyright infringement, for breach of the obligations of a confidential disclosure agreement, or even for breach of a previously granted license agreement. The presence of such claims confers several advantages.

First, it sharply reduces the probability that the defendant will succeed in avoiding a trial. Most defendants initially react to a suit by loudly and belligerently asserting that the case is without merit—that the patent is invalid and, even if it is valid, it is not infringed—and that the court will dismiss the suit (in some cases, these assertions are actually made in good faith). If pendant claims are present, a defendant that succeeds in establishing patent invalidity or noninfringement is still faced with the prospect of trial with respect to the other claims. This factor alone may cause a defendant to consider settlement more seriously.

Second, it is obvious that the greater the number of claims presented, the greater the probability that the plaintiff will prevail with respect to at least one of them. Finally, and perhaps most importantly, the presence of pendant claims may allow the plaintiff to introduce evidence casting the defendant in an unfavorable light. A trial (especially a jury trial) is, to a considerable extent, a morality play—an episode in the continuing struggle between good and evil. Quite early in a trial, a jury decides which party is the "good guy" and which is the "bad guy." All evidence presented thereafter is considered, evaluated, and accepted or rejected in the context of this decision.

While a jury may not fully understand the finer points of patent law (who does?), it is comfortable with the more universal concepts of lying, stealing, and taking unfair advantage. It is on this basis that a jury will ultimately render its verdict. If one of the universe of potential defendants has engaged in extensive communications with the patentee, inquired about product enhancements or further developments, or inquired about a possible license, that is the defendant of choice. Stated succinctly, choose the defendant against which success is most likely.

Other infringers that should be considered as candidates for a starring role in early litigation are those undergoing reorganization—acquisitions, mergers, spin-offs, divestitures, leveraged buyouts, public offerings, and so on—where the risks and distractions of litigation would be particularly unwelcome. These conditions often motivate a defendant to settle. Similarly, companies in weak financial condition or those committed to risky and expensive projects may also be inclined to settle. However, it is extremely frustrating to prevail at trial or secure a favorable settlement only to have the victory obviated by the bankruptcy of the defendant. Weak is good; too weak is not good—another example of the value of good intelligence.

Like war, patent enforcement may be defensive or offensive in nature. Defensive patent enforcement is directed to the protection of the monopoly supposedly secured by the patent-in-suit. It seeks to eliminate infringers who are poaching in the patented preserve. Offensive patent enforcement is most often directed to the extraction of value from otherwise unexploited (noncore) patents. It seeks to recover royalties from those using the subject inventions. Less often, offensive patent enforcement comprises an attempt to break into a protected market by attacking and overcoming the guardian patent through a declaratory judgment action.

## Developing a Strategy

Given that strategy is the plan for reaching an objective, the first step in developing a strategy is to clearly define the objective. Defining the objective too narrowly may lead to faulty strategy. For example, the objective of defensive patent enforcement may be to maintain an effective monopoly in the field of the patented invention. Obviously, obtaining a permanent injunction barring further infringement of the patent accomplishes this objective. Consider, however, an infringer for whom use of the patented invention is vital; for example, it is necessary for production of the infringer's only product. Imposition of an injunction, coupled with a refusal to subsequently grant a license in respect of the patent-in-suit, might well have a fatal impact on the infringer—it might put such an infringer out of business. Faced with such a catastrophic possibility, the infringer would have no choice but to fight to the bitter end. Such a reaction is clearly not to the advantage of the patentee. The infringer might succeed in proving the patent-in-suit invalid, unenforceable, or not infringed. Even if the patentee ultimately prevails in court, the costs of the matter may render the victory Pyrrhic at best.

If, however, the objective of the defensive enforcement is viewed not as securing an injunction, but as profit maximization (the ultimate objective of all business strategies), a new solution is possible—namely, licensing the infringer. By adding to the infringer's cost, the patentee retains a competitive advantage in the relevant market and receives a royalty, while avoiding the costs and risks of litigation to the death. If such an objective is, indeed, viable, the patentee could pursue a more flexible strategy of litigating to the point of maximum advantage—the point beyond which the costs of further litigation exceed the benefits derived therefrom—and then settling.

Determining the point of maximum advantage requires a careful analysis of the value actually being derived from the patent monopoly. Often, the result of such an analysis is surprising. For example, where the patentee lacks the resources to completely satisfy the demand for the patented product or service and does not foresee obtaining those resources in the near future, the presence of another supplier in the market may not result in lost sales and, indeed, may not even result in any price erosion. In such event, it would be advantageous to convert an infringer to a licensee, rather than wasting resources in seeking an injunction. Similarly, it may be determined that the market for the patented product or service is segmented; and that the infringer is positioned in a segment that is not presently addressed by the patentee nor likely to be so addressed in the near future. In such situations, the license will not only comprise a revenue source, but more importantly, may be used as a tool to prevent the former infringer from expanding into the market segment occupied by the patentee.

## Patent Reexamination—To Reexamine or Not to Reexamine, That Is the Question

Patent reexamination is, in essence, a procedure for removing uncertainty as to the validity of claims of an issued patent and for correcting claims that would otherwise be invalid. The procedure is available to all —patentees as well as third parties. The reexamination procedure allows a patent examiner to reopen the prosecution of the patent to consider prior art that had not been considered prior to issue.

Until recently, all patent reexamination was *ex parte*—anyone could initiate a reexamination, but only the patentee could communicate with the patent examiner after the process had commenced. This ability to respond to the examiner, indeed to bring substantial resources to bear, without any reply from a third-party petitioner, gave the patentees a decided advantage. Moreover, if possible, the same examiner who originally examined and allowed the patent to issue performs the reexaminations. Thus, to a degree, rejection of patent claims during reexamination required the examiner to admit having previously erred (to err is human, to admit it is uncommon). As a result of these factors, approximately 70% of reexamined claims survived reexamination, without the need for any amendment.

More importantly, once prior art had been cited to the Patent Office as the basis for a reexamination and successfully overcome by the patentee, its value as a basis of attacking the validity of the patent at trial was, for all practical purposes, destroyed. If a patent examiner has found the patent valid a second time (a so-called twice-blessed patent), neither a judge nor a jury is likely to find to the contrary.

Thus, if on the eve of filing suit or (after suit has been filed) during pretrial discovery, potentially invalidating prior art is uncovered, what is to be done? Should reexamination be sought? The answer to that question (like many legal questions) is, "It depends."

Given the aforementioned reexamination advantage, the patentee, under these circumstances, may well opt for reexamination. Indeed, where the defendant (or prospective defendant) is relying primarily on the defense of patent invalidity, a successful reexamination may induce settlement.

When the defendant asks the same question, the answer is not as clear. The facile response, of course, is that if reexamination favors the patentee, it should not be sought by the accused infringer. In actuality, the decision is not quite so simple; it may well depend on whether the accused has other, effective responses to the charge of infringement—invalidity due to prior sale or public use, failure to disclose the best mode of practicing the invention, lack of enablement, or noninfringement—that can be presented to a trier of fact. If such other defenses exist, the accused may well decide to accept the procedural handicap and present the highly technical, complex arguments as to invalidity to a patent examiner who is trained to understand them. If these arguments succeed and the patent claims are rejected as unpatentable in view of the newly cited prior art, the accused has prevailed. If the patent claims survive reexamination, the accused still may present to a judge or jury those other defenses that are more comprehensible to the layman.

Recent amendments to the patent law have created a second type of reexamination that (in theory) will eliminate the advantage presently enjoyed by the patentee. The new form of reexamination, known as an *inter partes* proceeding, allows the reexamination petitioner (the party that initiated the reexamination) to participate in the reexamination. The new procedure is available only with respect to patents issued on applications filed on or after November 29, 1999. No *inter partes* reexaminations have as yet been undertaken, and, indeed, final procedural rules have not yet been promulgated. It is clear, however, that the petitioner will be allowed to submit written comments with respect to each of the patentee's communications with the patent examiner responsible for the reexamination.

This ability to participate is the good news for a defendant or prospective defendant. The bad news is that, having initiated an *inter partes* reexamination, the petitioner will be estopped (barred or prevented) from presenting at a subsequent trial any defense that was raised or *could have been raised* during the reexamination. It remains to be seen how serious an effect this provision will have. Indeed, at this point, the tactical implications of *inter partes* reexamination remain unclear.

## Trial versus Settlement

Litigation involves risk—lots of it. Litigation, especially patent enforcement litigation, is very expensive. These are two good reasons to consider settlement rather than trial.

Historical data indicates that the odds are on the side of the patentee in a patent infringement suit. This is well and good; but, before drawing too much comfort from such data, you should consider the true nature of these statistics. They are an example of the Law of Large Numbers. (For those who are mathematically challenged, the Law of Large Numbers essentially states that as the number of events increases, the actual results will converge on the mathematically calculated results.) Thus, historical data provide a good prediction of the cumulative results of a large number of events. They do not provide nearly as good an indication of the result of the next single event. If a large number of cases are to be litigated, the results will likely approximate the historical statistics for such litigation. However, few patentees litigate a large number of cases. Most patentees will litigate one or, at most, a few cases. For these patentees, the historical data may have limited relevance.

For example, let us assume that one wishes to play Russian Roulette (a good analogy to patent enforcement trials). Mathematics tells us that, in any single game, the odds are five to one that the hammer will fall on an empty chamber. If the game is played six times, the odds are that the player will lose only once. However, it is just as likely that the loss will occur on the first game as on the second game, or on the third game, and so on. A player who loses the first game never gets to play again. The typical patentee, trying a suit for patent infringement, is in much the same situation. If the patent is held invalid or unenforceable (i.e., dead), there will be no more trials. If the patent is found valid and enforceable, but not infringed, the patentee may well lack sufficient resources (money) to try a second suit against a different infringer.

Most inventors are justifiably proud of their inventions. Some inventors are blinded by their pride. They will insist that a jury is certain to comprehend the merits of their inventions. *Do not listen to such people.* While it is true that historical data indicates that juries have somewhat of a pro-patent bias, juries are unpredictable. Post-trial discussions with jurors, or studies of so-called mock or shadow juries, consistently show that juries often reach their decisions based on matters considered trivial or even irrelevant by both plaintiff and defendant. This is especially true when neither side can present a clearly more sympathetic image than the other and the case is to be decided on purely technical (i.e., boring) grounds. If one can't entertain the jury or garner their sympathy, one can't count on their support. The same applies to judges. However well versed in the law, precious few judges ever studied the sciences or engineering. The more complex (incomprehensible) the technology of a case, the less likely the case will be decided on technological grounds. In many cases, going to trial is a poor (here, a euphemism for "dumb") risk-management technique.

Settlement avoids risk. It keeps the decision making in the hands of (supposedly) knowledgeable and educated executives, rather than in the hands of 12 bored jurors who generally are angry that they have been dragooned into jury duty. Settlement saves costs and avoids the distractions engendered by litigation. More importantly, litigation has few possible outcomes, while settlements can be structured to meet the peculiar needs of the parties. Finally, settlement tends to bring an end to the hostilities engendered by litigation. Think carefully before deciding to "roll the dice" because, to an unhappy extent, that is what occurs at trial. If you wish to gamble, go to a casino, where at least the drinks are free.

# Alternative Dispute Resolution

## Blessed Are the Peacemakers

It should be apparent to the reader that patent enforcement litigation is, at best, costly, time consuming, and distracting. (If it is *not* apparent, reread the "Patent Infringement" section of this chapter.) Fortunately, there are other avenues to the resolution of patent disputes, known collectively as *alternative dispute resolution.*

Although an infinite number of variations exist (and new ones are constantly being proposed), the different forms of alternative dispute resolution may be loosely categorized in three classes:

**1.** Mediation

**2.** Arbitration

**3.** Private trial

Mediation involves the introduction of a neutral third party who seeks to facilitate agreement between the disputants. It is quick and inexpensive. Success at resolution through mediation, however, is largely dependant on the interpersonal skills, experience, creativity, and professional stature of the mediator. While a mediator cannot force the parties to settle, a mediator whose opinions are highly valued and, hence, accepted by both disputants, may succeed in bringing them to a resolution. In general, however, mediation is not highly regarded, as the success rate is low. It seems to work best when it is truly voluntary and when the participants have full settlement authority, including sufficient rank and discretion that they needn't subsequently explain themselves to others. If these twin conditions are not satisfied, what ensues is merely a conclave of sullen flunkies whose only goal is to gather intelligence of their opponent's case, while disclosing none of their own. Mediation may be sought at any time, even during litigation (most commonly after discovery has been completed). This is, in fact, encouraged by the courts (judges do not find patent infringement trials entertaining).

Like mediation, arbitration involves the introduction of a neutral third party (most often a group of three neutral parties) into the dispute. Yet, where a mediator seeks to facilitate resolution, an arbitrator imposes one. Arbitration is final in that it is, for all practical purposes, unappealable. Arbitrators are not required to state the reasons or basis for their decision, nor are they obligated to follow the law, either statutory or precedential, substantive or procedural (hence the term, an *arbitrary decision*). Thus, in many respects, arbitration is even more unpredictable than litigation. There seems to be, however, a noticeable tendency on the part of arbitrators to "split the baby," giving something to each party. Finally, although arbitration is less costly and time consuming than litigation, it is far from rapid or inexpensive. Arbitration does, however, often yield a certain equality—leaving both parties equally angry and frustrated.

Private trial is the least utilized and most varied category of alternative dispute resolution devices. At one extreme, the parties retain a retired judge, who tries the case exactly as if it were being prosecuted within the judicial system. Because the judge has only one case on his or her docket, the matter progresses much more rapidly than it would had it been brought to court. At the other extreme, in the so-called mini-trial, each side is given a limited period of time (commonly half a day) to present its case, after which the judge, or sometimes a panel of judges, renders a decision. Private trials offer the considerable advantage of a reasoned opinion. However, since the decision is unappealable, the possession of a written opinion may be of little consolation to the losing party. Private trials are comparatively quick and economical, especially the mini-trial, although the degree of formality (along with the cost and duration) tends to increase in proportion to the stakes at risk.

An interesting combination of the private trial and mediation involves a mini-trial attended by one or more executives from each of the disputing parties. At the close of the case, the judge attempts to mediate a settlement by the attending executives. Often, the mini-trial hearing is the first time that senior executives have heard a full, uninterrupted, and unfiltered presentation of their opponent's case. Such a hearing may have a powerful impact on those who previously had been led to believe that the opposing case was meritless.

Whatever the approach selected, alternative dispute resolution can be tailored to meet the needs and desires of the parties involved. Moreover, it is private. It creates no transcript and no precedent (although documents produced may be subject to discovery in subsequent litigation).

# Summary

A patent claim is infringed when each of the claim limitations is found in the accused device or process. Infringement may be either literal or under the doctrine of equivalents. Literal infringement occurs when the claim language literally reads on the accused device or process. If a claim limitation is not literally met, but the corresponding structure in the accused device performs substantially the same function, in substantially the same way, to achieve the same result, the claim may be infringed under the doctrine of equivalents.

One who actively induces infringement of a patent is liable as an infringer. One who sells a component of a patented invention, knowing the component to be a nonstandard item especially adapted for use in an infringement of the patent, is liable as a contributory infringer.

The chief limitation on the doctrine of equivalents is file wrapper estoppel, which prevents recapturing, through a broad interpretation of claim language, scope that was surrendered during prosecution of the patent application. The recent decision in the *Festo* case has retroactively eliminated all equivalents of any claim limitation that was amended during prosecution.

Patent litigation involves the risks that the patent(s)-in-suit will be found to be invalid, unenforceable, or not infringed. Moreover, it is possible that a prevailing patentee will recover less than the costs of the litigation.

Suit may be brought only in a court that has jurisdiction over both the subject matter of the litigation (subject matter litigation) and the person of the defendant (personal jurisdiction). Personal jurisdiction may be based on the defendant's place of residence or, in some circumstances, on the defendant's actions (long-arm jurisdiction). In addition, suit may be brought only in the proper venue, which is that court, or courts, among all those having jurisdiction, where the rules provide that the case may be heard. Choice of venue may have a significant impact on the cost and outcome of litigation.

Generally speaking, plaintiffs in patent infringement lawsuits should demand a jury, rather than a bench trial, as they thereby have a greater chance of prevailing.

A party that has standing may bring an action, called a declaratory judgment (D.J.) action, seeking to have a patent held invalid, unenforceable, or not infringed. Standing is essentially a reasonable belief of an imminent suit for infringement by a patentee. Such a belief may arise out of communications from the patentee to a possible infringer.

A prevailing plaintiff in a patent infringement action may be awarded, as damages, either lost profits or a reasonable royalty. Lost profits are the incremental profits that would have been earned by the patentee if the patentee had made the sales that were, in fact, made by the infringer. A reasonable royalty is the royalty that would have been agreed on, by a willing licensor and a willing licensee, at the time the infringement began.

A prevailing patentee should consider damages resulting from price erosion (i.e., the need to reduce prices to compete with an infringer). In addition, the effect of the infringement on the sales of associated products or services should be considered. Sales of these products or services are known as convoyed sales, and consideration of these sales is known as the entire market value rule.

Patent infringement litigation, like all civil litigation, is commenced by the service of a summons and complaint. Thereafter, the defendant files an appearance and an answer and, generally, files affirmative defenses and counterclaims.

Claim construction is now a matter of law to be decided by the trial judge at a so-called Markman hearing, which is most commonly held after the pleadings are closed and a limited amount of discovery, directed to claim construction, has been had.

Two of the most common responses to a charge of patent infringement are (1) "I invented the accused product myself," and (2) "I purchased the accused product from another." Neither response is legally sufficient.

Laches and estoppel are two commonly encountered legal defenses. Both relate to a failure to take reasonably prompt action against known infringers. Laches bars recovery of past damages. Estoppel, which involves an affirmative act by the patentee that leads the accused infringer to believe it will remain unmolested, bars any recovery by the patentee.

When seeking legal representation, a law firm should be selected on the basis of its quality, flexibility, and price.

There are three basic approaches to attorney compensation: fixed fees, time-based billing, and contingency fees. Fixed fees are virtually never found in patent infringement cases. When using time-based billing, insist on detailed bills specifying the tasks performed, the amount of time devoted to each task, and the timekeeper(s) who performed each task (so-called task-based billing). Contingency fees are often subject to negotiation.

Patent enforcement is often a campaign against an industry. In such cases, a first defendant must be selected. Several factors should be considered when making this selection: a party's strength and ability to mount a strong defense; a party's past history—whether they settle or fight vigorously; the presence of so-called pendant claims—claims, other than patent infringement, that arise out of the same activity by the party; and a party's engagement in activities such as mergers, acquisitions, spin-offs, divestitures, and so on, which would constitute a distraction and might incline the party to settle any litigation.

Litigation requires a strategy, which, in turn, requires a clearly defined objective. Defining the objective too narrowly can result in faulty strategy by foreclosing otherwise advantageous resolutions or settlements.

Reexamination of a patent is a procedure whereby prosecution is reopened to allow the patent examiner to consider prior art not considered during the original prosecution. Uncertainty as to the validity of a patent, in light of newly discovered prior art, can often be resolved by reexamination.

The risks and costs inherent in litigation may be avoided by settlement. Additionally, the parties may structure a settlement to meet their peculiar needs.

In lieu of litigation, the parties may elect alternative dispute resolution. The various types of alternative dispute resolution may be divided into three loose categories: mediation, arbitration, and private trials.

# CHAPTER 9

# Intellectual Property in Cyberspace

## After reading this chapter you will be able to:

- Understand the special problems posed by business method patents and e-commerce
- Understand the relation of domain names to trademarks
- Understand the particular copyright problems presented by the Internet

## Business Method Patents and E-Commerce

Intellectual property in cyberspace is, essentially, the same as intellectual property in the real, brick and mortar world, where corporations are managed by adults and have earnings. The reader need not fear—everything (hopefully) learned from the preceding chapters, and (again, hopefully) to be learned from the succeeding ones, also applies to the new economy. A patent is still a patent, although the courts have now reinterpreted the patent system to cover a heretofore unpatentable variety of subject matter—the business method patent. A trademark is still a trademark, albeit issues may arise with respect to conflicting domain names. And a copyright is still a copyright (much to the chagrin of the folks at Napster).

It had long been considered axiomatic, by patent attorneys and agents, that neither algorithms nor methods of doing business were patentable. This belief, which was surprisingly lacking in precedential support, was recently laid to rest by the Court of Appeals for the Federal Circuit (CAFC) (*State Street Bank & Trust Co. v. Signature Financial Group, Inc.*, 149 F.3d 1368 [Fed. Cir. 1998]). Now, business methods are patentable, although no one seems able to agree on a definition of the term, least of all Congress. The American Inventors Protection Act gives the public certain prior use rights with respect to business method patents, without precisely identifying those patents to which it applies (see Exhibit 9.1). Basically, however, the term encompasses three broad categories:

**1.** Patents directed to the use of computers to perform traditional business functions

### EXHIBIT 9.1

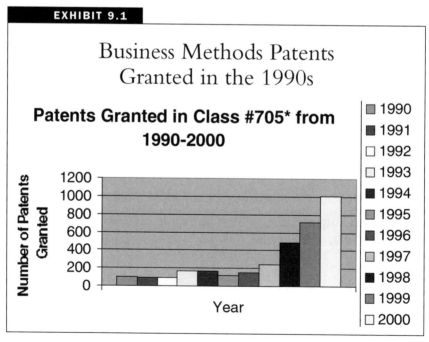

# Business Methods Patents Granted in the 1990s

**Patents Granted in Class #705* from 1990-2000**

*Class #705 includes patents for data processing: financial, business practice, management, or cost/price determination.

2. The so-called e-commerce category—patents directed to inventions pertaining to the Internet and electronic commerce

3. Patents directed to new methods of doing business that do not necessarily involve computers or the Internet

## Tradition, Tradition!

Traditionally, scientists and engineers who had become familiar with the patent system's requirements as to the best mode and an enabling disclosure (through continued exposure to the patent system) were the ones who created patentable inventions. (If the terms *best mode* and *enabling disclosure* seem unfamiliar, see Chapter 1).

These scientists and engineers generally were familiar with the pertinent prior art. Often, they were employed by business organizations that had created forms and procedures for disclosing new inventions; sometimes, these organizations even had an in-house patent department. Almost invariably, the inventors were able to provide plans, drawings, circuit diagrams, chemical formulae, and so on, to an attorney charged with preparing a patent application. Not uncommonly, prototypes had been built, and test results were available. All of these factors combined to maximize the quality of the resultant patent applications, while facilitating their preparation and, hence, minimizing their cost. None, or few, of these factors are present with respect to business method inventions.

Business method inventions are frequently created by first-timers—people, such as computer programmers, salesmen, and marketing personnel, who have not previously had any contact with the patent system. Often, they are employed (*if* they are employed) by organizations that are, themselves, first-timers and that can provide no institutional support. The inventors of business method inventions seem always to be in a hurry. Rather like Alice's rabbit, they are in much too much of a hurry to stop and describe their invention to an attorney. They don't know or can't be bothered to describe the prior art (no invention is an island—there is *always* prior art). They really haven't worked out all the details of their invention (these are generally "big picture" people) but assume that a few words and, perhaps, a sketch, will suffice. Often, it does suffice—the attorney spins straw into gold and completes a patent application. Such spinning, however, is time consuming and, therefore, costly (again, if this doesn't sound familiar, reread Chapter 1). The cost of preparing a business method patent application is typically about $15,000 (not including filing fees, amendments, issue fees, maintenance fees, automatic transmission, or white-wall tires).

## Problems, Problems, Problems

One of the first, and arguably the most important, steps in the examination of a patent application is the patent examiner's search for pertinent prior art. It is this prior art against which the examiner will assess the novelty and nonobviousness of the claimed invention. The examiner must base all decisions as to patentability of the invention on published documents—what "everyone knows" is not considered, only what someone published. To find these documents, examiners rely on the Patent Office search files—a voluminous collection of documents carefully arranged according to subject. Because they are in a convenient format and are already categorized in accord with the Patent Office system, the vast majority of the documents in the search files are earlier-issued patents. Thus, as a practical matter, the examiner's search, with respect to an application undergoing examination, is a search for previously issued patents in that field of technology.

Generally, the system functions well, but not in the case of business method patents. Until recently, there were no business method patents. Hence, there were no earlier-issued ones in the search files when the examiners performed their searches. The result: The earliest applications for these patents, filed after the State Street Bank decision opened the floodgates, sailed through the Patent Office to issue. Many of these patents are, to say the least, of questionable validity (a fact known to many in the industry). The Patent Office, having recognized the problem, has taken substantial steps to address it. A database has been created of various nonpatent documents, such as technical reports, product literature, and papers presented at meetings of professional associations, pertaining to this field; yet, even this effort has only ameliorated but not solved the problem because much of what was previously done was never openly documented. Since business methods were believed to be unpatentable—and at the time, they were—no one bothered to record and publish the results of their labors. Thus, the problem persists, albeit in a somewhat reduced degree, and criticism continues to be leveled at business method patents.

Another problem pertains to the scope of the patents. Even if (a very big if) they are valid, they are often narrow in scope. To a great extent, this is because many (if not most) business method patents rely on computer processing: Steps are performed by computers, which can, at very little cost, be reprogrammed so as to achieve substantially the same result through an entirely different procedure. Not only does this weakness reduce the value of the patent as a tool for securing a marketplace monopoly, it also limits the value of the patent as a tool for securing royalties through licensing to others. The cost of designing around the patent sets an upper limit on the amount of royalties a licensee would be willing to pay.

Ironically, another problem may arise if the patent does enable its owner to completely dominate a particular technology. The nature of e-commerce is such that the profitability of participation in a market is sometimes dependent on the efforts of others who develop and make available to consumers additional applications and variations of a basic technology. If a patentee exercises too much control of a technology, these others may simply turn to an alternate technology, leaving the patentee to dominate a barren and dying market. It has, for example, been suggested that Sony exercised too much control over the Beta videotape technology, causing its competitors to turn to the alternate VHS. In the end, the more widely available VHS became the popularly accepted standard, while Beta lapsed into consumer obscurity. Similarly, a newly developed computer system is unlikely to be widely purchased unless and until there is a broad variety of compatible software available. These considerations must be borne in mind when licensing strategies are being developed.

If business method patents are so expensive and suffer from such infirmities, why are they so popular? The answer, again, rests largely on the nature of e-commerce, populated as it is by many fledgling businesses (Is that a proper description for an activity with no revenues, nevermind no profits?) with no assets beyond an idea or a concept. If such businesses (hobbies, social clubs?) are to raise capital, it can be only on the basis of their intellectual property. There must be a patent or a pending patent application to exhibit to venture capitalists or prospective shareholders. Indeed, given the short life span of such technologies and the long periods of pendency in the Patent Office (currently well in excess of three years for business methods patents), patent applications may be nearly as valuable and effective as issued patents.

Finally, for all its shortcomings, a business method patent does confer a first-mover advantage. Even if it can be circumvented or shown to be invalid, it may secure for the patentee a window of opportunity in which to establish itself in the marketplace.

## Trademarks and Domain Names

Domain names are, in simple terms, the telephone numbers of the Internet. They allow us to send and receive messages (e-mail) and to reach desired web sites (information, products and services, advertising, and pornography). Like telephone numbers, domain names must be unique. However, unlike telephone numbers, domain names are not a standard number of digits (10, including the area code) assigned, seemingly at random, by the local telephone company. Rather, a company or other user chooses a name and applies to the Internet Corporation for Assigned Names and Numbers (ICANN) for registration. Unless the identical (and we do mean *identical*) name is already registered, the application will be granted.

Given virtually complete freedom to choose a domain name, most individuals and organizations select names that are easy to remember and are readily identified with their owners. Businesses, in particular, often choose names that comprise or incorporate their best-known trademarks or service marks. Sometimes, however, a business notices, to its chagrin, that its mark, or one confusingly similar thereto, has already been used in a domain name registered to another. Occasionally (actually, rarely), this is mere coincidence. More often, it is the prelude to what amounts to an attempt at extortion, when the registrant offers to sell the registration (prices in the range of $10,000 to $50,000 have been typical).

This type of activity, known as cybersquatting, is now prohibited by the Anticybersquatting Consumer Protection Act (ACPA), which bars the registration, transfer, or use of a domain name that is identical or confusingly similar to the trademark of another, or which dilutes a famous mark, when such activity is done in bad faith. Those who believe that they are the victims of cybersquatting can have recourse to the federal courts, where they may seek to recover the domain name owner's profits, actual damages, and costs. The Act does, however, also include an interesting antibullying provision. If a trademark owner knowingly misrepresents that a domain name is infringing or diluting its mark, the trademark owner may be held liable for resultant damages suffered by the domain name owner. To facilitate the resolution of disputes, ICANN has instituted an arbitration procedure whereby a trademark owner may object to the registration of a domain name by another; when successful, the contested domain name registration is canceled or assigned to the trademark owner.

# Copyright and the Internet

In our legal system, "the law" comprises not only statutes but also the decisions of the various courts that have applied the statutes to the facts presented by cases being heard (*stare decisis*). Each succeeding court decision, interpreting and defining the statutes or previous court decisions, in turn becomes part of the body of the law. While new statutes are enacted or old ones are amended only infrequently, court decisions are constantly adapting the law to meet the needs of our ever-evolving world. Nowhere is this practice more visible than in regard to the application of the copyright law (Title 17, United States Code) to the new, exciting (lawyerspeak for "opportunity to charge a lot") and challenging (lawyerspeak for "opportunity to *really* charge a lot") problems presented by the Internet.

## Copyright and Web Pages

As the reader should expect, web pages, like any original work of authorship, are protectable under the copyright law. Every time a page is downloaded from a web site, a copy of it (probably several copies of it) is made in the user's computer. Permission of the copyright holder is required before this can be done. The problem of securing such permission is compounded by the fact that a single web page may include articles (works) by different authors; hence, there are often several copyright holders from whom authorization to copy may be required.

Arguably, when material is placed on the web, webmasters intend that it should be downloaded, even if this is not explicitly stated. Such an intent may evidence an implied license to download. Nevertheless, who wants to rely on "may," especially when it is not clear that the webmaster had the authority to give such permission in the first place?

While most web site owners would complain about copying, others may complain about linking because it burdens their servers. Does placing of a link from one site to another constitute copyright infringement? Although the law is still unclear on this issue, it seems to be moving toward "yes." Although most links are unlikely to arouse the wrath of the copyright owner, several caveats are warranted.

Direct links to content that would normally be framed elsewhere are apt to cause objections. At present, there is little precedent on this issue because the few parties involved in such disputes have settled them. Still, if a linking page surrounds another's material with its own ads, cuts out another's ads, or makes it appear that the linking site is the source of the linked material, trouble is likely. Moreover, consider situations in which linked material infringes another's copyright. Most commonly, a copyright holder would act (threaten, sue, or assault) against only the party responsible for the directly infringing page; others linked to the infringing page would remain unaffected (probably even unaware of the infringement). However, where a direct infringer is beyond the effective reach of local courts and particularly where a site owner actively encourages use of an offending page, there may well be action taken against the owner of the linked site.

## Copyright and Electronic Publishing

Electronic publishing encompasses not only CD-ROM and related technologies but also online publishing.

CD-ROM and related technologies are much more analogous to classic publishing than online publishing. The CD-ROM involves the electronic compilations of text and images on a physical storage medium and the delivery of that storage medium to a buyer through channels of distribution that are virtually identical to the channels used to distribute conventional books.

Online publishing is generally accomplished by placing text and images on the Internet, with access being somehow limited. Most commonly, the users of the information are required to accede (or surrender, bow down, or roll over and play dead) to a license with a lot of small print enumerating all the things the buyer can and (mostly) cannot do with the material that has been purchased. In any event, these licensing contracts are helpful in combating the principal problem plaguing purveyors of CD-ROMs and online materials—people who form purchasing groups to buy works and share (lay term meaning "to infringe the copyright of") them.

## Copyright and Video Streaming

Copyright protection has long been the anchor that justified the billions of dollars spent to produce movies, television shows, and just about anything else involving video programming. Now the ability to turn anything into a digital video file means that anyone can create a perfect copy, throw it onto the Internet, and become a global pirate. The situation, which some claim could ruin the business model that makes all of this content possible in the first place, has already proven vexing.

Indeed, for big media companies, their entire library of past and future content is literally on the line, as in "online." And it is becoming increasingly difficult to determine what fees should be paid and when. Take digital music, which cable operators hope will give consumers yet another reason to want a broadband connection. The MP3 format, for example, yields about one megabyte of music per minute. That means that the typical pop song could take an hour or so to download using a 56 kilobits-per-second modem. And that's on a good day. But this potential bonanza for cable operators has its copyright complications. For example, music royalties can be broken down into two primary types: performance and mechanical. Performance royalties are paid into a copyright pool when, for instance, a song is played in a public place such as a bar or restaurant. But mechanical royalties go directly to artists and record companies based on actual product sales.

How will cable operators and programmers divide licensing fees and advertising revenue in the Internet age, much less figure out copyright issues?

These central questions surround any type of digital streaming of content. For now, it's an issue of the PC versus the TV. But in the future, copyright royalty collection will become even more complicated as interactive TV platforms proliferate.

## Copyright and Music on the Internet

The rapidly advancing technology of the Internet has spawned a plethora of legal entanglements as users explore the limits of the medium in the purchase and exchange of music. The latest war being raged in this arena is that over the MP3.

MP3 stands for MPEG1 (Moving Picture Experts Group 1), audio layer 3, and is a technique designed to compress bulky files of digitized music to facilitate ease of download and storage for bandwidth- and disk-space-starved music fans. Unlike its precursors, such as RealAudio, MP3 compression technology allows one to quickly download near-CD quality digitized sound recordings and to store them using minimal disk space. To copyright holders, this technology presents the threat of users being able to compile enormous libraries of pirated songs and to store them indefinitely, using only a small fraction of their hard drives. The files can also be easily attached to e-mail and sent to any number of friends or uploaded to other web sites.

The real threat to the recording industry, as the issue has been cast thus far, is that each successive copy is *identical to the original*; there is no loss in fidelity no matter the generation of the copy. It was precisely for this reason that the recording industry so vehemently opposed the introduction of DAT technology in the late 1980s and succeeded in the passage of the Audio Home Recording Act of 1992. Back in the days when the worst damage a wannabe music pirate could inflict was to dub his Aerosmith cassette and make copies for his friends, the industry did not worry as much about serial copying of copyrighted music. The marginal cost of making copies was constricted by the price of cassette tapes—not expensive, but enough to limit truly mass-scale copying for all but the most dedicated—and each successive copy was of poorer quality than the last. There was little market for a second-, third-, or fourth-generation scratchy home recording.

With the advent of MP3 and related technologies, that has all changed. The Internet music industry is predicted to hit $1.6 billion by 2002 and somewhere in the vicinity of 500,000 MP3 files out there on the web. Granted, making and listening to MP3 files requires a computer and software, but the software is available for download from the Internet for free, along with simple instructions for its use. In addition, electronics hardware manufacturers have been quick to introduce portable MP3 players, which can be used to play the music anywhere, eliminating the need to sit at one's computer in order to listen to the music.

Largely due to this ease of transmission and use, an underground movement in pirated MP3 files has grown. Some speculate that more than 90% of MP3 files currently in circulation were obtained without the copyright owner's permission. The industry has responded by waging an all-out war on MP3 files, constantly monitoring the web for signs of insurgence and sending cease and desist letters to the operators of infringing sites. Record companies are also trying to shut the system down at the source by filing suit against manufacturers of MP3 players, considering action against search engines that help find MP3 files, lobbying for favorable legislation, and working feverishly to develop a competing proprietary standard that can be more easily managed.

This war has largely been cast as a battle between the industry on one side and the artists and their fans on the other. Artists claim that the current system whereby they receive only pennies on the dollar for CD sales is archaic and that the Internet now provides a distribution medium that allows them to distribute their songs directly to their fans, cutting out the middleman. Music fans insist that paying $17.99 for a CD, which costs a small fraction of that to make, is a rip-off, and they cite the low royalties to artists as another reason for their ire. In some convolution of logic akin to a shoplifter's justification of only stealing from big businesses, they seem to be saying that it is okay to take the music because the sellers are making too much money from them. The backup argument when this one fails is that they *would* buy MP3 files, if only the record companies would make them available for purchase. Since they don't, the only way to get their favorite tracks on MP3 is through piracy.

## Summary

Intellectual property in cyberspace is much like intellectual property in more traditional businesses. Many of the problems associated with business method patents arise out of the fact that the prior art in this field was never documented and is not available to patent examiners during examination of business method patent applications. Although this problem has been somewhat ameliorated, many of the earliest-issued business method patents are of questionable validity.

Domain names are the telephone numbers of the Internet. Most individuals and businesses choose names that are readily identified with their owners. Some unscrupulous individuals seek to extort money by obtaining domain names that would be associated with famous individuals or businesses, a practice known as *cybersquatting*. Statutes have been enacted to prevent this. Copyright law is constantly evolving in response to new problems presented by the Internet. Partly as a result, the law in this area is rather unsettled.

# CHAPTER 10

# The Patent Portfolio and Its Effect on Stock Price

## After reading this chapter you will be able to:

- Identify the firms in an industry that are likely to experience the greatest increase in value

- Recognize three figures of merit useful in analyzing patent portfolios and their potential impact on stock price

It is generally believed—or hoped—that research and development (R&D) expenditures by a business corporation will lead to increased profits and, ultimately, to an increase in the value of the corporation and the price of its stock. Empirical research tends to support this belief. It should be apparent, however, that all such expenditures do not produce equal results. Some R&D programs are technologically successful, while others are not. Some programs are focused on areas of declining interest or value, producing only incremental improvements to mature technologies, while other programs are pioneering efforts in promising new fields. Some otherwise successful R&D efforts result in products that are market failures.

The task therefore is to ascertain the value, as opposed to the cost, of a firm's intellectual assets, in such a manner as to provide an indicator of future stock appreciation. If this can be done, based on publicly available information (the SEC is really cracking down on insider trading), one can attempt to forecast future stock performance and pick the winners. (*Question:* How can one leave Wall Street with a small fortune? *Answer:* Enter Wall Street with a large fortune.) Somewhat surprisingly, the necessary information is at hand, although it requires a little familiarity with patents and a considerable amount of compiling and massaging.

A very good picture of an organization's intellectual assets may be derived from an examination of its patent portfolio. By now, the reader should be aware that this information can be compiled from public records of the Patent Office, or online. The question therefore reduces to one of analyzing patent portfolios to determine which firms will experience the greatest increase in stock price. In essence, we need to identify some predictive portfolio characteristic or quality, so-called figures of merit. Fortunately, several such figures of merit have been developed and empirically tested by Baruch Lev, professor at the New York University School of Economics, and others. These portfolio characteristics include: patent count, citation impact, and science linkage.

## Patent Count

As the reader is undoubtedly aware, all patents are not equal. Some are much more valuable than others. Nevertheless, individual differences tend to be of less importance as the size of a portfolio increases (the law of large numbers rears its head once more). Thus, the number of patents in a firm's portfolio, the patent count, may be taken as an indicator of the intensity and the success rate of the firm's R&D activities. Within an industry, the relative size of a firm's patent portfolio, as compared to other firms in the same industry, has been found to correlate well with that firm's future ratio of stock price to book value (the SP/BV ratio). Within an industry, the firms that have the greatest number of patents tend to have the highest SP/BV ratio. With over 30,000 patents in its portfolio, IBM holds the title as the world's largest single patent holder.

# Citation Impact

Accepting that some patents are more valuable than others, in terms of their potential impact on future profitability, how do we identify these more valuable patents? The short answer to this question is that others have already identified them for us.

On the cover sheet of each U.S. patent is a listing of the prior art references cited during the course of the patent's prosecution. These references are categorized as: U.S. patents, foreign patents, and nonpatent publications. By examining these citations, which may now be done by computer, it is possible to determine whether (or how often) a patent of interest has been cited as prior art with respect to succeeding patents. The presence of such citation suggests that the citing patent pertains to technology that, in some way, is an improvement or refinement of the technology of the cited patent.

The existence of a number of patents wherein the patent of interest is cited as a prior art reference suggests that: (1) the cited patent pertains to a basic invention; and (2) that this basic invention is in a field that is of significant interest to others in the industry. Indeed, it may well be that the cited patent dominates some or all of the citing patents. Remember the red fire engine. The more often a patent is cited as a prior art reference in later-issued patents, the greater the probability that the cited patent is a basic and, hence, valuable patent. We may therefore take it as a sign of merit or predictor of relative future profitability when the patents in the portfolio of one firm are more often cited in later-issued patents than are the patents in the portfolios of other firms in the same industry. In other (simpler) words, the firm whose patents are cited as prior art most often is likely to be the most profitable in the future.

# Science Linkage

In citation impact, we are concerned with forward citation, which is the citation of the patent of interest as a prior art reference in later-issued patents. Science linkage is a tool that employs backward citation, which is an examination of the prior art references cited in the patent of interest.

It is generally accepted (a phrase used in academia meaning "you'll have to trust us on this, because we can't prove it") that basic research yields a higher return (up to three times as high) than product development. How, then, does one determine whether a patent pertains to a basic research invention or a (probably less valuable) product development invention? An imperfect but workable solution is to count the number of scientific papers cited as prior art references. The underlying theory is that the greater the number of such citations, the closer the patented invention is to basic science (whatever that is). Thus, if the patents in the portfolio of one firm have, on average, more citations to nonpatent scientific papers than the patents in the portfolios of other firms in the same industry, it is likely that that firm will exhibit greater profitability, in the future, than the industry average.

There are, of course, significant limitations to the use of the foregoing figures of merit. They are applicable only to firms that have patent portfolios of statistically significant size—probably a minimum of about 40 patents. Also, they are suitable only for comparison of firms within a single industry. They do not provide meaningful results in comparing firms in different industries. Nevertheless, they do comprise a means of ranking the firms in an industry with respect to their projected relative profitability.

# Summary

Corporate R&D efforts, if successful, lead to an increase in value of the corporation and the price of its stock. However, not all research efforts are successful or of equal impact on a firm's future earnings. Empirical data supports the use of three figures of merit as valid predictors of future profitability of a firm as compared to others in the same industry.

Patent count, which is the relative size of a firm's patent portfolio as compared to other firms in the industry, has been found to correlate well with that firm's future profitability.

Citation impact, which is a measure of the frequency with which the patents of one firm are cited in later issued patents of others, is an indication of how basic is the firm's technology. The more often its patents are so cited, the more basic and valuable its technology is likely to be.

Science linkage is a measure of the frequency with which scientific articles are cited as prior art in a firm's own patents. The higher a firm's science linkage, the closer its technology is to basic research, as opposed to product development. Patents pertaining to basic research are, generally, more valuable than patents on product developments.

# Trademark and Service Mark Application

This form and the instructions for its use are available on the United States Patent and Trademark Office (USPTO) web site at *http://www3.uspto.gov/teas/PrintV1.22/TFORMWIN.htm.*

ESSENTIALS of Intellectual Property

| Applicant Information | | |
|---|---|---|
| * Name | | |

**Entity Type:** Click on the **one** appropriate circle to indicate the applicant's entity type and enter the corresponding information.

| | | |
|---|---|---|
| ○ Individual | Country of Citizenship | |
| ○ Corporation | State or Country of Incorporation | |
| ○ Partnership | State or Country Where Organized | |
| | Name and Citizenship of all General Partners | |
| | Specify Entity Type | |
| | State or Country Where Organized | |
| ○ Other | * Street Address | |
| | * City | |
| | State | Select State ▾  <br> If not listed above, please select 'OTHER' and specify here: [ ] |
| | * Country | Select Country ▾  <br> If not listed above, please select 'OTHER' and specify here: [ ] |
| | Zip/Postal Code | |
| Phone Number | | |
| Fax Number | | |
| Internet E-Mail Address | ☐ Check here to authorize the USPTO to communicate with the applicant or its representative via e-mail. NOTE: While the application may list an e-mail address for the applicant, applicant's attorney, and/or applicant's domestic representative, **only one** e-mail address may be used for correspondence, in accordance with Office policy. The applicant must keep this address current in the Office's records. | |

## Mark Information

Before the USPTO can register your mark, we must know exactly what it is. You can display a mark in one of two formats: (1) typed; or (2) stylized or design. When you click on one of the two circles below, and follow the relevant instructions, the program will create a separate page that displays your mark once you validate the application (using the Validate Form button at the end of this form). You must print out and submit this separate page with the application form (even if you have listed the "mark" in the body of the application). If you have a stylized mark or design, but either you do NOT have a GIF or JPG image file or your browser does not permit this function, check the box to indicate you do NOT have the image in a GIF or JPG image file (and then see the special help instructions).

**WARNING:** AFTER SEARCHING THE USPTO DATABASE, EVEN IF YOU THINK THE RESULTS ARE "O.K.," DO NOT ASSUME THAT YOUR MARK CAN BE REGISTERED AT THE USPTO. AFTER YOU FILE AN APPLICATION, THE USPTO MUST DO ITS OWN SEARCH AND OTHER REVIEW, AND MIGHT REFUSE TO REGISTER YOUR MARK.

| * Mark | **Typed Format** | Click on this circle if you wish to register a word(s), letter(s), and/or number(s) in a format that can be reproduced using a typewriter. Also, only the following common punctuation marks and symbols are acceptable in a typed drawing (any other symbol, including a foreign diacritical mark, requires a stylized format): . ? " - ; ( ) % $ @ + , ! ' : / & # * = [ ] Enter the mark here: NOTE: The mark **must** be entered in ALL upper case letters, regardless of how you actually use the mark. E.g., MONEYWISE, **not** MoneyWise. |
| | **Stylized or Design Format** | Click on this circle if you wish to register a stylized word(s), letter(s), number(s), and/or a design. Click on the 'Browse' button to select GIF or JPG image file from your local drive that shows the complete, overall mark (i.e., the stylized representation of the words, e.g., or if a design that also includes words, the image of the "composite" mark, NOT just the design element). Do NOT submit a color image. ☐ Check this box if you do NOT have the image in a GIF or JPG image file. For a stylized word(s) or letter(s), or a design that also includes a word(s), enter the LITERAL element only of the mark here: |
| Additional Statement | | This section is for the entry of various statements that may pertain to the mark. In no case must you enter any of these statements for the application to be accepted for filing (although you may be required to add a statement(s) to the record during the actual prosecution of the application). To select a statement, check the box and enter the specific information relevant to your mark. The following are the texts of the most commonly asserted statements: |

☐ **DISCLAIMER:** "No claim is made to the exclusive right to use ___ apart from the mark as shown."

☐ **STIPPLING AS A FEATURE OF THE MARK:** "The stippling is a feature of the mark."

☐ **STIPPLING FOR SHADING:** "The stippling is for shading purposes only."

☐ **PRIOR REGISTRATION(S):** "Applicant claims ownership of U.S. Registration Number(s) ___."

☐ **DESCRIPTION OF THE MARK:** "The mark consists of ___."

☐ **TRANSLATION:** "The foreign wording in the mark translates into English as ___."

☐ **TRANSLITERATION:** "The non-Latin character(s) in the mark transliterate into ___, and this means ___ in English."

☐ **§2(f), based on Use:** "The mark has become distinctive of the goods/services through the applicant's substantially exclusive and continuous use in commerce for at least the five years immediately before the date of this statement."

☐ **§2(f), based on Prior Registration(s):** "The mark has become distinctive of the goods/services as evidenced by the ownership on the Principal Register for the same mark for related goods or services of U.S. Registration No(s). _____."

**§2(f), IN PART, based on Use:** "_____ has become distinctive of the goods/services through the applicant's substantially exclusive and continuous use in commerce for at least the five years immediately before the date of this statement."

**§2(f), IN PART, based on Prior Registration(s):** "_____ has become distinctive of the goods/services as evidenced by the ownership on the Principal Register for the same mark for related goods or services of U.S. Registration No(s). _____."

**NAME(S), PORTRAIT(S), SIGNATURE(S) OF INDIVIDUAL(S):**

○ "The name(s), portrait(s), and/or signature(s) shown in the mark identifies _____, whose consent(s) to register will be submitted.

○ "The name(s), portrait(s), and/or signature(s) shown in the mark does not identify a particular living individual.

**USE OF THE MARK IN ANOTHER FORM:** "The mark was first used anywhere in a different form other than that sought to be registered on _____, and in commerce on _____."

**CONCURRENT USE:** Enter the appropriate concurrent use information, e.g., specify the goods and the geographic area for which registration is sought.

## BASIS FOR FILING AND GOODS AND/OR SERVICES INFORMATION

Applicant requests registration of the trademark/service mark identified above with the Patent and Trademark Office on the Principal Register established by the Act of July 5, 1946 (15 U.S.C. §1051 et seq.) for the following Class(es) and Goods and/or Services, and checks the basis that covers those specific Goods or Services. More than one basis may be selected, but do **NOT** claim both §§1(a) and 1(b) for the identical goods or services in one application.

**Section 1(a), Use in Commerce: Applicant is using or is using through a related company the mark in commerce on or in connection with the below identified goods and/or services. 15 U.S.C. § 1051(a), as amended. Applicant attaches or will submit one specimen for** *each class* **showing the mark as used in commerce on or in connection with any item in the class of listed goods and/or services. If filing electronically, applicant must attach a JPG or GIF specimen image file for each international class, regardless of whether the mark itself is in a typed drawing format or is in a stylized format or a design. Unlike the mark image file, a specimen image file may be in color (i.e., if color is being claimed as a feature of the mark, then the specimen image should show use of the actual color(s) claimed).**

Describe what the specimen submitted consists of:

| International Class | |
|---|---|
| | If known, enter class number 001 - 042, A, B, or 200 |

| | |
|---|---|
| * Listing of Goods and/or Services<br><br>**USPTO Goods/Services Manual** | |
| Date of First Use of Mark Anywhere | at least as early as:<br><br>MM/DD/YYYY |
| Date of First Use of the Mark in Commerce | at least as early as:<br><br>MM/DD/YYYY |

**Section 1(b), Intent to Use:** Applicant has a bona fide intention to use or use through a related company the mark in commerce on or in connection with the goods and/or services identified below (15 U.S.C. §1051(b)).

| | |
|---|---|
| International Class | If known, enter class number 001 - 042, A, B, or 200 |
| * Listing of Goods and/or Services<br><br>**USPTO Goods/Services Manual** | |

**Section 44(d), Priority based on foreign filing:** Applicant has a bona fide intention to use the mark in commerce on or in connection with the goods and/or services identified below, and asserts a claim of priority based upon a foreign application in accordance with 15 U.S.C. §1126(d).

| | |
|---|---|
| International Class | If known, enter class number 001 - 042, A, B, or 200 |
| * Listing of Goods and/or Services<br><br>**USPTO Goods/Services Manual** | |
| Country of Foreign Filing | Select Country ▼<br><br>If not listed above, please select 'OTHER' and specify here: |

| Foreign Application Number | |
|---|---|
| | NOTE:If possible, enter no more than 12 characters. Eliminate all spaces and non-alphanumeric characters. |
| Date of Foreign Filing | |
| | MM/DD/YYYY |

☐ Section 44(e), Based on Foreign Registration: Applicant has a bona fide intention to use the mark in commerce on or in connection with the above identified goods and/or services, and submits or will submit a certification or certified copy of the foreign registration before the application may proceed to registration, in accordance with 15 U. S.C. 1126(e), as amended.

| International Class | If known, enter class number 001 - 042, A, B, or 200 |
|---|---|
| * Listing of Goods and/or Services  **USPTO Goods/Services Manual** | |
| Country of Foreign Registration | Select Country ▾  If not listed above, please select 'OTHER' and specify here: |
| Foreign Registration Number | |
| | NOTE:If possible, enter no more than 12 characters. Eliminate all spaces and non-alphanumeric characters. |
| Foreign Registration Date | MM/DD/YYYY |
| Renewal Date for Foreign Registration | MM/DD/YYYY |
| Expiration Date of Foreign Registration | MM/DD/YYYY |

☐ Check here if an attorney is filing this application on behalf of applicant(s). Otherwise, click on Domestic Representative to continue.

## Attorney Information

| Correspondent Attorney Name | |
|---|---|
| Individual Attorney Docket/Reference Number | |
| Other Appointed Attorney(s) | |
| Attorney Address | Street Address | |
| | City | |

198

| State | Select State ▼ |
|---|---|
| | If not listed above, please select 'OTHER' and specify here: ☐ |
| Country | Select Country ▼ |
| | If not listed above, please select 'OTHER' and specify here: ☐ |
| Zip/Postal Code | |
| Firm Name | |
| Phone Number | |
| FAX Number | |
| Internet E-Mail Address | ☐ Check here to authorize the USPTO to communicate with the applicant or its representative via e-mail. NOTE: While the application may list an e-mail address for the applicant, applicant's attorney, and/or applicant's domestic representative, **only one** e-mail address may be used for correspondence, in accordance with Office policy. The applicant must keep this address current in the Office's records. |

☐ Check here if the applicant has appointed a Domestic Representative. **A Domestic Representative is REQUIRED if the applicant's address is outside the United States.**

## Domestic Representative

The applicant must appoint a Domestic Representative if the applicant's address is outside the United States. The following is hereby appointed applicant's representative upon whom notice or process in the proceedings affecting the mark may be served.

| Representative's Name | | |
|---|---|---|
| Address | Street Address | |
| | City | |
| | State | Select State ▼ |
| | | If not listed above, please select 'OTHER' and specify here: ☐ |
| | Zip Code | |
| Firm Name | | |
| Phone Number | | |
| FAX Number | | |
| Internet E-Mail Address | | ☐ Check here to authorize the USPTO to communicate with the applicant or its representative via e-mail. NOTE: While the application may list an e-mail address for the applicant, applicant's attorney, and/or applicant's domestic representative, **only one** e-mail address may be used for correspondence, in accordance with Office policy. The applicant must keep this address current in the Office's records. |

## Fee Information

**Number of Classes Paid**

1

**Note:** The total fee is computed based on the Number of Classes in which the goods and/or services associated with the mark are classified.

$ 325 = **Number of Classes Paid x $325 (per class)**

\* **Amount**

$

## Payment

☐ **Deposit Account Number**
(If checked, please enter six numbers with no space or hyphen).

The U.S. Patent and Trademark Office is hereby authorized to charge any fees or credit any overpayments to the deposit account listed above.

**Name of Person authorizing account activity**

**Company/Firm Name**

### Declaration

The undersigned, being hereby warned that willful false statements and the like so made are punishable by fine or imprisonment, or both, under 18 U.S.C. §1001, and that such willful false statements may jeopardize the validity of the application or any resulting registration, declares that he/she is properly authorized to execute this application on behalf of the applicant; he/she believes the applicant to be the owner of the trademark/service mark sought to be registered, or, if the application is being filed under 15 U.S.C. §1051(b), he/she believes applicant to be entitled to use such mark in commerce; to the best of his/her knowledge and belief no other person, firm, corporation, or association has the right to use the mark in commerce, either in the identical form thereof or in such near resemblance thereto as to be likely, when used on or in connection with the goods/services of such other person, to cause confusion, or to cause mistake, or to deceive; and that all statements made of his/her own knowledge are true; and that all statements made on information and belief are believed to be true.

Signature _____ Date Signed _____

Signatory's Name

Signatory's Position

# Copyright Application

This form and many other copyright forms, along with instructions for their use, are available on the U.S. Copyright Office web site at *http://www.loc.gov/copyright/forms/*.

FEE CHANGES

Fees are effective through June 30, 2002. After that date, check the Copyright Office Website at www.loc.gov/copyright or call (202) 707-3000 for current fee information.

**FORM TX**
For a Nondramatic Literary Work
UNITED STATES COPYRIGHT OFFICE

REGISTRATION NUMBER

_____

TX _____ TXU _____
EFFECTIVE DATE OF REGISTRATION

_____

Month _____ Day _____ Year

**DO NOT WRITE ABOVE THIS LINE. IF YOU NEED MORE SPACE, USE A SEPARATE CONTINUATION SHEET.**

# 1

TITLE OF THIS WORK ▼

_____

PREVIOUS OR ALTERNATIVE TITLES ▼

_____

PUBLICATION AS A CONTRIBUTION If this work was published as a contribution to a periodical, serial, or collection, give information about the collective work in which the contribution appeared.    Title of Collective Work ▼

If published in a periodical or serial give: Volume ▼    Number ▼    Issue Date ▼    On Pages ▼

# 2    a

NAME OF AUTHOR ▼

DATES OF BIRTH AND DEATH
Year Born ▼    Year Died ▼

Was this contribution to the work a "work made for hire"?
☐ Yes
☐ No

AUTHOR'S NATIONALITY OR DOMICILE
Name of Country
OR { Citizen of ▶ _____
Domiciled in ▶ _____

WAS THIS AUTHOR'S CONTRIBUTION TO THE WORK
Anonymous?    ☐ Yes ☐ No
Pseudonymous?  ☐ Yes ☐ No
If the answer to either of these questions is "Yes," see detailed instructions.

NATURE OF AUTHORSHIP Briefly describe nature of material created by this author in which copyright is claimed. ▼

**NOTE**

Under the law, the "author" of a "work made for hire" is generally the employer, not the employee (see instructions). For any part of this work that was "made for hire" check "Yes" in the space provided, give the employer (or other person for whom the work was prepared) as "Author" of that part, and leave the space for dates of birth and death blank.

b

NAME OF AUTHOR ▼

DATES OF BIRTH AND DEATH
Year Born ▼    Year Died ▼

Was this contribution to the work a "work made for hire"?
☐ Yes
☐ No

AUTHOR'S NATIONALITY OR DOMICILE
Name of Country
OR { Citizen of ▶ _____
Domiciled in ▶ _____

WAS THIS AUTHOR'S CONTRIBUTION TO THE WORK
Anonymous?    ☐ Yes ☐ No
Pseudonymous?  ☐ Yes ☐ No
If the answer to either of these questions is "Yes," see detailed instructions.

NATURE OF AUTHORSHIP Briefly describe nature of material created by this author in which copyright is claimed. ▼

c

NAME OF AUTHOR ▼

DATES OF BIRTH AND DEATH
Year Born ▼    Year Died ▼

Was this contribution to the work a "work made for hire"?
☐ Yes
☐ No

AUTHOR'S NATIONALITY OR DOMICILE
Name of Country
OR { Citizen of ▶ _____
Domiciled in ▶ _____

WAS THIS AUTHOR'S CONTRIBUTION TO THE WORK
Anonymous?    ☐ Yes ☐ No
Pseudonymous?  ☐ Yes ☐ No
If the answer to either of these questions is "Yes," see detailed instructions.

NATURE OF AUTHORSHIP Briefly describe nature of material created by this author in which copyright is claimed. ▼

# 3    a

YEAR IN WHICH CREATION OF THIS WORK WAS COMPLETED This information must be given ◀ Year in all cases.

b Complete this information ONLY if this work has been published.

DATE AND NATION OF FIRST PUBLICATION OF THIS PARTICULAR WORK
Month ▶ _____ Day ▶ _____ Year ▶ _____ ◀ Nation

# 4

COPYRIGHT CLAIMANT(S) Name and address must be given even if the claimant is the same as the author given in space 2. ▼

See instructions before completing this space.

TRANSFER If the claimant(s) named here in space 4 is (are) different from the author(s) named in space 2, give a brief statement of how the claimant(s) obtained ownership of the copyright. ▼

APPLICATION RECEIVED

ONE DEPOSIT RECEIVED

TWO DEPOSITS RECEIVED

FUNDS RECEIVED

DO NOT WRITE HERE
OFFICE USE ONLY

**MORE ON BACK ▶**  • Complete all applicable spaces (numbers 5-9) on the reverse side of this page.
• See detailed instructions.    • Sign the form at line 8.

DO NOT WRITE HERE
Page 1 of _____ pages

# Copyright Application

| EXAMINED BY | FORM TX |
|---|---|
| CHECKED BY | |
| ☐ CORRESPONDENCE  Yes | FOR COPYRIGHT OFFICE USE ONLY |

**DO NOT WRITE ABOVE THIS LINE. IF YOU NEED MORE SPACE, USE A SEPARATE CONTINUATION SHEET.**

**5**

**PREVIOUS REGISTRATION** Has registration for this work, or for an earlier version of this work, already been made in the Copyright Office?
☐ Yes  ☐ No  If your answer is "Yes," why is another registration being sought? (Check appropriate box.) ▼
a. ☐ This is the first published edition of a work previously registered in unpublished form.
b. ☐ This is the first application submitted by this author as copyright claimant.
c. ☐ This is a changed version of the work, as shown by space 6 on this application.
If your answer is "Yes," give: **Previous Registration Number** ▶            **Year of Registration** ▶

**6**  **a**

**DERIVATIVE WORK OR COMPILATION**
**Preexisting Material** Identify any preexisting work or works that this work is based on or incorporates. ▼

See instructions before completing this space.

**b**

**Material Added to This Work** Give a brief, general statement of the material that has been added to this work and in which copyright is claimed. ▼

**7**  **a**

**DEPOSIT ACCOUNT** If the registration fee is to be charged to a Deposit Account established in the Copyright Office, give name and number of Account.
**Name** ▼                              **Account Number** ▼

**b**

**CORRESPONDENCE** Give name and address to which correspondence about this application should be sent.   Name/Address/Apt/City/State/ZIP ▼

Area code and daytime telephone number ▶                          Fax number ▶
Email ▶

**8**

**CERTIFICATION*** I, the undersigned, hereby certify that I am the
Check only one ▶
☐ author
☐ other copyright claimant
☐ owner of exclusive right(s)
☐ authorized agent of _____
Name of author or other copyright claimant, or owner of exclusive right(s) ▲

of the work identified in this application and that the statements made by me in this application are correct to the best of my knowledge.

Typed or printed name and date ▼ If this application gives a date of publication in space 3, do not sign and submit it before that date.
_____  Date ▶ _____

Handwritten signature (X) ▼
X _____

**9**

| Certificate will be mailed in window envelope to this address: | Name ▼ |
|---|---|
| | Number/Street/Apt ▼ |
| | City/State/ZIP ▼ |

**YOU MUST:**
• Complete all necessary spaces
• Sign your application in space 8

**SEND ALL 3 ELEMENTS IN THE SAME PACKAGE:**
1. Application form
2. Nonrefundable filing fee in check or money order payable to *Register of Copyrights*
3. Deposit material

**MAIL TO:**
Library of Congress
Copyright Office
101 Independence Avenue, S.E.
Washington, D.C. 20559-6000

As of July 1, 1999, the filing fee for Form TX is $30.

# Confidentiality and Nondisclosure Agreement

**THIS AGREEMENT** is made the __ day of _____, 20__, by and between _____, a ____[company type, e.g., a corporation] organized and existing under the laws of the State of _____, having a principal place of business at _____ ("Disclosing Party"), and _____, [company type, if applicable] [organized and existing under the laws of the State of _____, if applicable], having a principal place of business at [if business, or] with offices at _____ ("Recipient").

**WHEREAS**, Disclosing Party is the proprietor of information concerning _____ (the "Information"); and

**WHEREAS**, Recipient is interested to learn the Information so as to be able to determine their interest in the use of the Information [or, in connection with _____ project].

**NOW, THEREFORE, in consideration of mutual premises and covenants** it is mutually agreed as follows.

1. Disclosing Party agrees to divulge to Recipient sufficient details of the Information to enable Recipient to understand the substance thereof. It is mutually understood that, unless otherwise specifically indicated in writing, any information so communicated by Disclosing Party to Recipient is confidential and constitutes valuable trade secrets of Disclosing Party.

2. In order to induce Disclosing party to divulge the Information, Recipient covenants and warrants (i) to use the Information only for the purposes hereinabove stated, (ii) not to use any of the Information for the Recipient's own benefit, and (iii) not to disclose any of it to third parties without the prior written permission of Disclosing Party.

205

3. Excluded from the above restriction is any part of Disclosing Party's disclosure that:
   a. can be demonstrated to have been in the public domain prior to the date hereof;
   b. can be demonstrated to have been in Recipient's possession prior to the date hereof.
   c. becomes part of the public domain by publication or otherwise, not due to any unauthorized act or omission on Recipient's part; or
   d. is supplied to Recipient by any third party as a matter of right insofar as the Information had been obtained by such third party lawfully.
4. The rights and obligations herein are personal to Disclosing Party and Recipient and cannot be assigned without the prior written permission of the other party. This Agreement contains the entire understanding of the parties relating to the matters referred to herein, and can only be amended by a written instrument duly executed on behalf of Disclosing Party and Recipient.

**IN WITNESS WHEREOF,** the parties hereto have caused this Agreement to be duly executed as of the date hereinabove set forth.

_____ **[The Disclosing Party]**

By: _____

Name, Title

_____ **[Recipient]**

By: _____

Name [Title, if applicable]

# Invention Assignment Form

[*Note:* This assignment may not provide an assignee the right to sue for and recover damages for acts of infringement occurring prior to the date of the assignment.]

**Practitioner's Docket No.**_____ *PATENT*

For:   [ ] U.S. and/or [ ] Foreign Rights
For:   [ ] U.S. Application or
          [ ] U.S. Provisional Application
For:   [ ] U.S. Patent
For:   [ ] PCT Application
By:   [ ] Inventor(s) or [ ] Present Owner

## ASSIGNMENT OF INVENTION

In consideration of the payment by ASSIGNEE to ASSIGNOR of the sum of One Dollar ($1.00), the receipt of which is hereby acknowledged, and for other good and valuable consideration,

**ASSIGNOR:**

Inventor(s) or person(s) or entity(ies)
who own the invention

_____

*(type or print name(s) of ASSIGNOR(S))*

_____

Address

_____

_____

Nationality

*(if assignment is by person or entity to whom invention was previously assigned and this was recorded in PTO, add the following)*

**Recorded on** _____     **Reel** _____

hereby sells, assigns and transfers to

**ASSIGNEE:**

_____

*(type or print name(s) of ASSIGNOR(S))*

_____

Address

_____

_____

Nationality

and the successors, assigns and legal representatives of the ASSIGNEE

*(complete one of the following)*

[ ] the entire right, title and interest

[ ] an undivided _____ percent (_____ %) interest

for the United States and its territorial possessions

*(check the following box, if foreign rights are also to be assigned)*

[ ] and in all foreign countries, including all rights to claim priority, in and to any and all improvements which are disclosed in the invention entitled:

_____

Name of inventor(s) _____

_____

*(check and complete (a), (b), (c), (d), (e), (f), or (g))*

and which is found in (37 C.F.R. § 3.21)

(a) [ ]    U.S. patent application executed on even date herewith

(b) [ ]    U.S. patent application executed on _____

(c) [ ]    U.S. provisional application naming the above inventor(s) for the above-entitled invention.

[ ] Express mail label no.: _____

Mailed: _____

[ ]  To comply with 37 CFR 3.21 for recordal of this assign-
     ment, I, an ASSIGNOR signing below, hereby authorize
     and request my attorney to insert below the filing date and
     application number when they become known.

(d) [ ]  U.S. application no. /_____ filed on
     _____

(e) [ ]  International application no. PCT /_____/_____ filed
     on _____

(f) [ ]  U.S. patent no. _____ issued _____
         [ ] A change of address to which correspondence is to be
             sent regarding patent maintenance fees is being sent
             separately.

*(also check (g), if foreign application(s) is also being assigned)*
(g) [ ]  and any legal equivalent thereof in a foreign country,
         including the right to claim priority
and, in and to, all Letters Patent to be obtained for said invention by the
above application or any continuation, division, renewal, or substitute
thereof, and as to letters patent any reissue or re-examination thereof.

ASSIGNOR hereby covenants that no assignment, sale, agreement
or encumbrance has been or will be made or entered into which would
conflict with this assignment.

ASSIGNOR further covenants that ASSIGNEE will, upon its
request, be provided promptly with all pertinent facts and documents
relating to said invention and said Letters Patent and legal equivalents as
may be known and accessible to ASSIGNOR and will testify as to the
same in any interference, litigation or proceeding related thereto and
will promptly execute and deliver to ASSIGNEE or its legal representatives any and all papers, instruments or affidavits required to apply for,
obtain, maintain, issue and enforce said application, said invention and
said Letters Patent and said equivalents thereof which may be necessary
or desirable to carry out the purposes thereof.

IN WITNESS WHEREOF, I/We have hereunto set hand and seal
this _____ day of _____.
    Date of signing

**WARNING:** *The date of signing must be the same as the date of execution of the application, if item (a) was checked above.*

Date: _____

**Signature of ASSIGNOR(S)**

Date: _____

Date: _____

Date: _____

*(if ASSIGNOR is a legal entity, complete the following information)*

_____

*(type or print the name of the above person authorized to sign on behalf of ASSIGNOR)*

_____

Title

**NOTE:** *No witnessing, notarization or legalization is necessary. If the assignment is notarized or legalized, then it will only be prima facie evidence of execution. 35 USC 261. Use next page if notarization is desired.*

[ ]    Notarization or Legalization Page Added.

# Basic IP Audit Questionnaire

1. List all patents and pending patent applications, domestic and foreign.
   Verify that:
   a. all patents and patent applications are properly assigned;
   b. all maintenance fees have been paid, and future payments have been docketed; and
   c. prosecution of all pending patent applications is current.

2. Does the organization have a procedure for recording and disclosing new inventions? If "no," institute invention disclosure procedure; if "yes," obtain list of all disclosed inventions.

3. List all trademark and service mark registrations and pending applications for registration, domestic and foreign.
   Verify that:
   a. all registrations and applications for registration are in the name of the organization or have been properly assigned;
   b. all affidavits of use and renewal applications have been filed; and
   c. prosecution of all pending applications is current.

4. List all unregistered trademarks and service marks used by the organization.

5. Collect and catalog copies of all publications, including catalogues, advertising and promotional materials, shareholder reports, etc.
   Check for:
   a. unlisted trademarks and service marks;
   b. proper trademark and service mark usage; and
   c. proper copyright notices.

6. List all copyright registrations. Verify that all registrations are in the name of the organization or have been properly assigned.

7. List all mask works. Verify that all mask works are registered in the name of the organization or have been properly assigned.

8. List all registered designs. Verify that all design registrations are in the name of the organization or have been properly assigned.

9. Does the organization possess any information that provides a competitive advantage with respect to its competitors? If "yes," verify that the information is marked "confidential," that access to such information is restricted, and that it is otherwise properly protected.

10. Have all employees executed appropriate Invention Assignment and Confidentiality Agreements? If "no," secure necessary agreements.

11. Are all consultants and independent contractors required to execute appropriate Invention Assignment and Confidentiality Agreements? If "no," institute appropriate procedure.

12. Obtain copies of all licenses of intellectual property in which the organization is a licensor or licensee.

13. List all lawsuits pertaining to intellectual property in which the organization is or was a party.

# Patent Valuation

## Portfolio Valuation

What is a patent worth? The answer depends on who is asking the question. Two things, however, should be apparent: The true nature of intellectual property is the additional or incremental value it brings to its owner; and the incremental value is dependent on the manner in that the property is used. There are, essentially, four scenarios in which a valuation of intellectual property is commonly sought:

1. The intellectual property may be owned by an individual or an enterprise that utilizes the property to maintain a monopoly with respect to a product it makes and/or sells, or a service it provides.

2. The intellectual property may be owned by an individual or an enterprise that does not utilize the property directly, but is willing to sell or license it to others.

3. An individual or enterprise may purchase intellectual property or take an exclusive license thereunder to avail itself of a public franchise afforded thereby.

4. An individual or enterprise may take a nonexclusive license of the intellectual property so as to be able to offer a new product or service in a competitive environment.

Let us consider each category separately.

Consider, for example, a pharmaceutical company selling a patented blockbuster drug. While the patent is active, the company enjoys a large market share and can charge for its drug whatever the market will bear. Once the patent expires (or is invalidated in court), a score of generic drug manufacturers enter the scene and the maker of the blockbuster drug inevitably suffers from price and market share erosion.

Thus, to such a company, a patent protecting a particular product or process[1] would be worth exactly the net present value of the difference between the revenues derived from the sales of this product or service, under the monopoly afforded by the patent and the corresponding revenues in an unpatented, freely competitive environment. Calculating the this difference on an annual basis, we have

$$1. \quad V(P) = \langle R \rangle \times \langle S \rangle - R \times S$$

where $V(P)$ is the annual value of the patent $P$; $\langle R \rangle$ is the price of the patented product or process in a given year; $\langle S \rangle$ is the market share during this year within the term of public franchise, expressed as the sales volume of the patented product (e.g., units); and $R$ and $S$ are respectively the price and the sales volume of the same product or process in the same year but without the benefit of the monopoly afforded by the patent (hypothetical values corresponding to a scenario in which there was no patent protection).

To obtain the total value of the patent over its statutory life we need to sum the expression by years—from the year the patent was issued (one can enjoy patent protection only from the date it is issued[2]) until it expires. Assuming that an active patent has $l$ years remaining in its term, we have

$$2. \quad V(P) = \sum_{i=1}^{l} \left( \langle R \rangle_i \times \langle S \rangle_i - R_i \times S_i \right)$$

where $\langle R \rangle_i, \langle S \rangle_i, \langle R \rangle_i$, and $\langle S \rangle_i$ are values as in expression (1) taken in a year $i$ and summed by $i$ from the year the patent issued until it expires.

Thus, the patent value is the sum of the incremental values of the public franchise on an annual basis over the life of the patent. Written in another way

$$3. \quad V(P) = \sum_{i=1}^{l} \Delta_i$$

where

$$4. \quad \Delta_i = \langle R \rangle_i \times \langle S \rangle_i - R_i \times S_i$$

Suppose the patent application had been pending in the Patent Office for four years, before it issued as a U.S. utility patent. Since the patent term is 20 years from the filing date, this patent (during its term) will afford its owner 16 years of public franchise. In this case, the expression (3) will look like

$$5. \quad V(P) = \left( \langle R \rangle_1 \times \langle S \rangle_1 - R_1 \times S_1 \right) + \left( \langle R \rangle_2 \times \langle S \rangle_2 - R_2 \times S_2 \right)$$

$$+ \ldots + \left( \langle R \rangle_{16} \times \langle S \rangle_{16} - R_{16} \times S_{16} \right)$$

or

$$6. \quad V(P) = \Delta_1 + \Delta_2 + \ldots + \Delta_{16}$$

In reality, the economic life of a product is often significantly less than the statutory term of the patent. Technological obsolescence, changing tastes, and other factors may shorten the economic life of the product. The average economic life of a patent (before the underlying technology becomes obsolete) is only about five years from the date of issue. In this case, the sum (5) will have fewer terms as the sales volume eventually dwindles to zero.

It is important to note that the annual incremental values $\Delta_i$ change over the life of the patent. Such changes may result, for example, from product promotion, the availability (and cost) of substitute products, and general economic conditions. All such factors must be taken into account when forecasting values for formula (3), and it must be done on an annual basis, as the relative impact of each of these factors may change from year to year.

The previous formulae define the value (i.e., the incremental revenues) of a patent over its entire statutory (or economic) life. In order to obtain the present value of the patent, we must discount the future incremental values $\Delta_i$:

$$7. \quad PV(P) = \sum_{i=1}^{l} \frac{\langle R \rangle_i \times \langle S \rangle_i - R_i \times S_i}{(1 + I_i)^i}$$

where $I_i$ is the discount interest rate in the year $i$.

In a simplified case similar to an ordinary annuity, where the incremental annual value of a public franchise $\Delta_i$ and the annual discount rate $I_i$ remain constant ($\Delta_i = \Delta$ and $I_i = I$) throughout the life of the patent, expression (7) can be written as

$$8. \quad PV(P) = \Delta \left[ \frac{1 - \left[ \dfrac{1}{(1 + I)^l} \right]}{I} \right]$$

For example, the present value of a patent, which secures a public franchise yielding a constant incremental annual value $\Delta$, with a remaining life of seventeen years ($l = 17$), and a discount rate of ten percent ($I = 0.10$) is

$$9. \quad PV(P) = \Delta \left[ \frac{1 - \left[ \dfrac{1}{1 + 0.1)^{17}} \right]}{0.1} \right] = 8.02\Delta$$

Thus for $\Delta = \$10,000,000$, the present value of the patent is $\$80,215,533^3$.

Formula (2) and the subsequent expressions have been derived under the assumption that the patented product is protected by one, and only one, patent. Nevertheless, these formulas also describe the value of an entire patent portfolio protecting a patented product or service. (A patent portfolio represents a group of patents protecting a revenue stream. This stream may be generated by a single product, a product line or by the enterprise as a whole.) Note that the value of the patent portfolio protecting a single product or service does not depend on the number of patents in the portfolio.

Thus, the value of a patent portfolio $V(PP)$ can be calculated as

$$10. \quad V(PP) = \sum_{i=1}^{I} \left( \langle R \rangle_i \times \langle S \rangle_i - R_i \times S_i \right)$$

or

$$11. \quad V(PP) = \sum_{i=1}^{I} \Delta_i$$

The present value is given by

$$12. \quad PV(PP) = \sum_{i=1}^{I} \frac{\langle R \rangle_i \times \langle S \rangle_i - R_i \times S_i}{\left(1 + I_i\right)^i}$$

or

$$13. \quad PV(PP) = \sum_{i=1}^{I} \frac{\Delta_i}{\left(1 + I_i\right)^i}$$

## Individual Patent Valuation

Let us assume that there are $n$ patents in the portfolio. One might think that the value of any patent in this portfolio is its *pro rata* share:

$$14. \quad V(P) \equiv \frac{1}{n} V(PP) = \frac{1}{n} \sum_{i=1}^{I} \left( \langle R \rangle_i \times \langle S \rangle_i - R_i \times S_i \right)$$

This, however, can be true only when all patents in the portfolio were issued on the same date and will expire on the same date in the future. In real life this rarely happens. To overcome this problem, we first note that

$$15. \quad V(PP) = \sum_{j=1}^{n} V(P_j)$$

where the value of a portfolio of $n$ patents is described as the sum of values of each individual patent $P_j$ in the portfolio. To account for the fact that the patents may be obtained and expire at different times, we have to consider the situation on an annual basis (with the simplifying assumption that all patents are obtained on the first day of a year and they expire on the last day of a year[4]). Thus, in any given year $i$ the annual value of the public franchise, and therefore the "annual" value of the patent portfolio, is

$$16. \quad \sum_{j=1}^{n} V(P_i^j) = \langle R \rangle_i \times \langle S \rangle_i - R_i \times S_i$$

The total value of the portfolio over its entire life is

$$17. \quad \sum_{i=1}^{l} \sum_{j=1}^{n} V(P_i^j) = \sum_{i=1}^{l} \left( \langle R \rangle_i \times \langle S \rangle_i - R_i \times S_i \right)$$

where $l$ is the total number of years of the portfolio.

Since addition is a commutative operation, expression (17) can be rewritten as

$$18. \quad \sum_{j=1}^{n} \sum_{i=1}^{l} V(P_i^j) = \sum_{i=1}^{l} \left( \langle R \rangle_i \times \langle S \rangle_i - R_i \times S_i \right)$$

or

$$19. \quad \sum_{j=1}^{n} V(P_j) = \sum_{i=1}^{l} \left( \langle R \rangle_i \times \langle S \rangle_i - R_i \times S_i \right)$$

$V(P_j)$ is the value of the $j$-th patent, $P_j$, over its life. Equation (19) gives the sum of values $V$ of all portfolio patents $P_j$. We need to solve this equation for $V(P_j)$. To do that, let us now assume that all active (issued and nonexpired) patents contribute equal value to the portfolio. We need to account for the fact that some of the patents may have been filed later than others and will expire later (or be invalidated earlier) than others. To do that, we shall introduce a matrix $\mathbf{P}$ (if the mathematical term matrix is unfamiliar to you, think of a table), where rows correspond to years of the portfolio's life and columns correspond to the individual patents in the portfolio. If a particular patent is active in a particular year we shall write into a corresponding cell of the matrix a positive number greater than 0, and less than or equal to 1; if the patent has not been issued yet or has already expired, we shall write "0". In other words, the matrix element $p_j^i$ is positive ($0 < p_j^i \leq 1$) when, and only when, the patent $j$ is active in the year $i$; otherwise, it is 0. Since the value of a patent portfolio does not depend on the number of its constituent patents, the values assigned to the individual cells of the matrix must satisfy a simple rule: The sum of all elements in any row of the matrix must be equal to one. We shall call this matrix $\mathbf{P}$ a *Patent Portfolio Weight Matrix*.

Let us, for example, consider a patent portfolio consisting of three patents over a period of four years. Let us assume that, during the first year, the portfolio consisted of only one patent $P_1$; during the second year, it consisted of two patents $P_1$ and $P_2$ (the second patent just issued); during the third year, there is only one patent $P_2$ (the first patent expired at the end of the second year); and during the fourth year there are two patents: $P_2$ and $P_3$. Let us insert these facts into the table:

| | Patent 1 | Patent 2 | Patent 3 |
|---|---|---|---|
| Year 1 | 1 | 0 | 0 |
| Year 2 | 0.5 | 0.5 | 0 |
| Year 3 | 0 | 1 | 0 |
| Year 4 | 0 | 0.5 | 0.5 |

Note that we have apportioned the values pro rata to the number of patents active that year. In years 2 and 4, there were two patents active, and we therefore assigned values of 0.5 to each patent in those years so as to satisfy our rule that the sum of row elements must be equal to 1. In other words, the value in a given cell is $1/n$, where n is the number of patents active that year.

Alternatively, in mathematical notation, the Patent Portfolio Weight Matrix **P** looks, in this case, as follows:

$$20. \quad P = \begin{pmatrix} 1 & 0 & 0 \\ 0.5 & 0.5 & 0 \\ 0 & 1 & 0 \\ 0 & 0.5 & 0.5 \end{pmatrix}$$

Generally, the Patent Portfolio Weight Matrix **P** gives a complete picture of what patents are active in any given year over the life of the portfolio.

We have assumed here that all patents in the portfolio were active throughout the entire year. This is an oversimplification, as patents may issue and expire at any time during the year. To account for this reality, instead of $1/n$, we can assign to an active patent a number weighted pro rata according to the number of months the patent was (or will be) active that year. For example, suppose that in the Patent Portfolio Weight Matrix (20) the second patent issued in the beginning of July. Then, instead of 0.5, we will assign a weighted number 0.25. This automatically raises the value of the first patent:

$$21. \quad P = \begin{pmatrix} 1 & 0 & 0 \\ 0.75 & 0.25 & 0 \\ 0 & 1 & 0 \\ 0 & 0.5 & 0.5 \end{pmatrix}$$

Our other assumption, that all of the patents contribute equally to the portfolio, led us to assign the same value to each patent active for a given number of months during that particular year. This need not be so. Patents may have different values. One would not, for example, assign the same value to a broad patent on a basic technology as one would assign to a narrow patent on a relatively minor improvement in the technology.

The litmus test in determining the relative values of the patents in a portfolio is to ask the following question: How much of the monopoly will be lost if this particular patent is removed from the portfolio (sold, expired, or invalidated)? The broader the scope of the patent claims, the broader the monopoly secured by the patent and, therefore, the larger the relative value of this patent to the portfolio. We always need to remember that a patent is a legal instrument and its value is strictly proportional to the legal protection it affords (i.e., the scope of the patent claims).

However, individual patents may change their value during their terms as well. For example, a patent, which emerges untarnished from Patent Office reexamination, with its presumption of validity enhanced, is now worth more than before. A patent that is ruled to be valid and enforceable (actually not *invalid* or *unenforceable*) in a court of law may grow in value even more. Conversely, a patent whose validity is challenged (e.g., by third party initiation of *ex parte* reexamination proceedings) is worth less for as long as its validity is in doubt.

The Patent Portfolio Weight Matrix allows us to account both for individual patents having different values, relative to each other, and for patents having a relative value which varies over the patent's life. To account for these differences, one needs to weigh or assess each patent during each year and to assign different numbers, slightly higher or lower values, to corresponding cells in the matrix **P**. In doing so, one must follow the same simple rule: *The sum of all values in every row must be equal to 1.* For example, if, during the second year, the first patent accounted for only 40% of the portfolio value that year, while the second patent accounted for the remaining 60%, we would rewrite the matrix (20) as

$$22. \quad P = \begin{pmatrix} 1 & 0 & 0 \\ 0.4 & 0.6 & 0 \\ 0 & 1 & 0 \\ 0 & 0.5 & 0.5 \end{pmatrix}$$

or, if the second patent only issues in July as in (21), we would have

$$23. \quad P = \begin{pmatrix} 1 & 0 & 0 \\ 0.7 & 0.3 & 0 \\ 0 & 1 & 0 \\ 0 & 0.5 & 0.5 \end{pmatrix}$$

Expression (23) describes a Patent Portfolio Weight Matrix **P** weighted with respect to individual patent contribution to the portfolio value, both over time and in relative value. Thus, the Patent Portfolio Weight Matrix **P** gives a complete picture of which patents are active in any given year over the life of the portfolio, as well as their relative value or weight.

Since the sum of all elements in any row is 1, the sum of all elements of the matrix is equal to the number of rows—the total number of years in the life of the portfolio (commencing with the issuance of the first patent and terminating at the end of the term of the last to expire patent). We will call this number a Portfolio Statutory Life, $L$. Generally, $L$ is the sum of all elements $p^j{}_i$ (or, simply, the number of the rows) of the matrix **P**:

$$24. \quad L = \sum_j \sum_i p_i^j$$

We will also introduce here a Patent Weight Index $p^j$ defined as the sum of the values in a $j$ column of the matrix $\mathbf{P}$:

$$25. \quad p^j = \sum_i^l p_i^j$$

Patent Weight Index $p^j$ is the sum of all weighted values for a given patent throughout the life of the portfolio. It is a weighted contribution of the individual patent to the portfolio. It is clear that the Portfolio Statutory Life $L$ is the sum of all Patent Weight Indexes $p^j$ for all constituent patents in the portfolio:

$$26. \quad L = \sum_j^n p^j$$

If the average value of a portfolio patent is $\overline{V}$, then the value $V(P^j)$ of an individual patent $P^j$ is the Patent Weight Index $p^j$ multiplied by the average value of an individual patent in the portfolio:

$$27. \quad V(P^j) = p^j \times \overline{V}$$

The value of a patent portfolio is the sum of values of the individual patents:

$$28. \quad V(PP) = \sum_{j=1}^n p^j \times \overline{V}$$

or

$$29. \quad V(PP) = L \times \overline{V}$$

Since, according to (10),

$$30. \quad V(PP) = \sum_{i=1}^l \left( \langle R \rangle_i \times \langle S \rangle_i - R_i \times S_i \right)$$

we have for the average value of a portfolio patent $\overline{V}$:

31. $\displaystyle \overline{V} = \frac{1}{L} \times \sum_{i=1}^{l} \left( \langle R \rangle_i \times \langle S \rangle_i - R_i \times S_i \right)$

Once we know the average patent value, substituting it in expression (27) gives us the value of an individual patent $P^j$:

32. $\displaystyle V\left(P^j\right) = \frac{1}{L} \times p^j \times \sum_{i=1}^{l} \left( \langle R \rangle_i \times \langle S \rangle_i - R_i \times S_i \right)$

or

33. $\displaystyle V\left(P^j\right) = \frac{1}{L} \times p^j \times \sum_{i=1}^{l} \Delta_i$

It is easy to see that for a patent portfolio consisting of a single patent, $p^j = L$ and the value of the patent is equal to the value of the portfolio. In the case of a portfolio consisting of no concurrent patents of equal value, $p^j/L = 1/n$ and the expression (32) reverts to (14), as expected.

The present value of a patent is given by the expression

34. $\displaystyle PV\left(P^j\right) = \frac{p^j}{L} \times \sum_{i=1}^{l} \frac{\langle R \rangle_i \times \langle S \rangle_i - R_i \times S_i}{\left(1 + I_i\right)^i}$

Or, as in the case of an ordinary annuity, where the incremental annual value of public franchise $\Delta_i$ and the annual discount rate $I_i$ remain constant ($\Delta_i = \Delta$ and $I_i = I$) throughout the life of the patent, the expression (34) can be written as

35. $\displaystyle PV\left(P^j\right) = \frac{p^j}{L} \times \Delta \left[ \frac{1 - \left[ \dfrac{1}{\left(1 + I\right)^l} \right]}{I} \right]$

# Mini-max Approach to Patent Valuation

In certain instances, it may be difficult to accurately forecast the parameters of expression (34) to calculate with precision the value of a patent. In such cases, it may be useful at least to ascertain the range of numbers that represent minimum and maximum values of the patent.

In determining the value of a patent it is important to remember that many patents can be designed around. This fact places an effective upper limit on the value of the patent. Indeed, any potential patent buyer or licensee faces a dilemma: (1) to buy or license a patent, or (2) to design around the patent. Thus, it appears that the maximum value of a patent is the cost of designing around:

$$36. \quad max(PV) = C_{da}$$

where $C_{da}$ is the cost of designing around the patent in question. Upon further consideration, we notice that the cost of designing around a patent is anything but certain. Therefore, we must allow for cost overruns, delays, and other factors that may ultimately increase the design around cost. We must further consider the possibility of failure of attempts to design around the patent. Should such an attempt fail, the resulting losses would be arguably equal to the maximum patent value (if we cannot design around the patent, we must buy it at a price equal to its maximum value). To account for all these factors, we rewrite (36) as

$$37. \quad max(PV) = C_{da} \times (1 + P_{co}) + P_f \times max(PV)$$

where $P_{co}$ is the probability of cost overruns and $P_f$ is the probability of design around failure. Even if the design around is successful, the patent owner will have the first-mover advantage. We therefore have

$$38. \quad max(PV) = C_{da}(1 + P_{co}) + P_f \times max(PV) + FMA$$

where *FMA* is the value of the first mover advantage. Solving this equation for the maximum patent value we have

$$39.\quad \max(PV) = \frac{C_{da} \times (1 + P_{co}) + FMA}{(1 - P_f)}$$

Expression (39) represents the maximum value of a patent. This result is based on the premise that the public franchise afforded by a patent cannot be worth more than the cost of legally circumventing the patent monopoly.

The minimum value of the patent can be gauged from two factors. First, when a patent application is first filed, a calculated decision has been made to trade the value of the trade secret related to the invention for the value of the patent protection. (In reality, such calculation is rarely done explicitly, though it certainly should be done.). This leads one to conclude that at the very least the patent should be worth as much as the trade secret (the price paid for obtaining the patent). The monopoly afforded by the trade secret is limited to the economic life of the underlying invention (which usually is shorter than the statutory life of a patent) and is further limited by the possibility that a competitor will discover the trade secret independently or reverse engineer that product. The last factor may limit the value of the trade secret to a first mover advantage.

## In the Real World

The previous formulae describe the present value of patents in an ideal world in which competitors respect the intellectual property rights of each other and do not infringe each other's patents. In the real world, where patent infringement is a commonplace reality, we must assume that patents will be challenged by an infringing competitor(s) and will need to be enforced in a court of law.

To adjust our formulae to this more realistic situation, we need to consider at least two additional factors: (1) the probability $E$ that the patent owner will, in the event of infringement, enforce its patent rights, and (2) the probability $F$ that the patent owner will prevail in court. With this in mind, we can now rewrite expressions (10) and (12) as follows:

$$40. \quad V(PP) = E \times F \times \sum_i \left( \langle R \rangle_i \times \langle S \rangle_i - R_i \times S_i \right)$$

and

$$41. \quad PV(PP) = E \times F \times \sum_{i=1}^{I} \frac{\langle R \rangle_i \times \langle S \rangle_i - R_i \times S_i}{(I + I_i)^i}$$

The probability $E$ that the patent owner, in the event of infringement, will enforce its patents depends mainly on two factors: one's willingness, $E_w$, and one's ability, $E_a$, to do so.

Needless to say, a patent portfolio owned by a company that is unlikely to enforce it is worth considerably less (if anything at all) than a similar portfolio owned by a company that vigorously enforces its patents, all other things being equal.

Another factor, not less important, that contributes to the probability of patent enforcement $E$, is the ability to enforce the patents $E_a$.

All these factors of willingness $E_w$ and ability $E_a$ must be taken into account when estimating the probability of patent enforcement $E$. Assuming, for simplicity, that these two factors are independent, the total probability of enforcement $E$ is the product of these two factors:

$$22. \quad E = E_w * E_a$$

If one is absolutely determined to enforce one's patent portfolio ($E_w = 1$), one can improve one's ability to enforce by purchasing an infringement abatement insurance policy, in which case $E_a = 1$.

The probability $F$ of prevailing at trial is also comprised of several factors, which include: (1) the probability $F_i$ that at least one of the patents in the portfolio will be found to be infringed; (2) the probability $F_v$ that at least one of the infringed patent(s) will be found valid; and (3) the probability $F_e$ that at least one of the infringed and valid patent(s) will be found enforceable.

Recent research shows that the statistical probability of these values is as follows: The probability $F_i$ that a given patent will be found infringed is 66%. The probability $F_v$ that a given patent will be found valid is 67%. The probability $F_e$ that a given patent will be found enforceable is 88%.

In the real world, the value of a patent portfolio increases with its size; since all patents must be found invalid to avoid infringement, the total probability of invalidating each individual patent is

$$42. \quad F_v = 1 - \prod_{j=1}^{n}\left(1 - F_v^j\right)$$

where the Greek symbol $\prod$ denotes multiplication by each patent $P^j$. Assuming, for simplicity, that all individual probabilities are equal ($F_v^j = F_v$), we have

$$43. \quad F_v = 1 - \left(1 - F_v^j\right)^n$$

The probability of invalidating an individual patent is 33%; this number falls off very rapidly as the number of patents increases. Thus, the probability of invalidating both patents of a two-patent portfolio is $0.33 \times 0.33 = 0.1$ (1%); the probability of invalidating all the patents in a 10-patent portfolio is entirely negligible at $0.33^{10} = 0.00001$ (one thousandth of 1%!).

Exactly the same situation is true with respect to the enforceability of patents. We have, therefore,

44. $F_e = 1 - \prod_{j=1}^{n}\left(1 - F_e^j\right)$

and, assuming for simplicity that all individual probabilities are equal ($F_e^j = F_e$), we have

45. $F_e = 1 - \left(1 - F_e^j\right)^n$

Since the probability $F_e$ that a patent will be found unenforceable is only 12%, this probability vanishes very rapidly as the number of patents increases. In a portfolio of just two patents, this probability is only 1.4%.

With respect to infringement, it is sufficient to prove that any one of the patents in the portfolio (even a single claim) is infringed to establish liability. Therefore, to avoid liability for infringement, the defendant would need to successfully defend against each asserted patent (strictly speaking, each asserted claim). Thus, the probability of noninfringement is the product of noninfringement probabilities for each individual patent:

46. $F_i = 1 - \prod_{j=1}^{n}\left(1 - F_i^j\right)$

and, again, assuming for simplicity that all individual probabilities are equal ($F_i^j = F_i$), we have

47. $F_i = 1 - \left(1 - F_i^j\right)^n$

When a patentee asserts only one patent, the chances of success in proving infringement are 66%; for two patents, the chances improve to 89%; and for five patents, the chances are better than 99.5%.

The previous calculations are all based on the assumption of event independence: in accordance with patent law, the questions of validity, enforceability, and infringement are decided independently for each patent. It is important to remember that in reality, human psychology plays a role equally important (or even more important) than the law during jury deliberations. Thus, juries (and, at times, even judges) tend to lump patents together, which destroys the assumption of event independence. In fact, judges rule in favor of the same party on both validity and infringement in 74% of the cases.[5] Juries rule in favor of the same party in 86% of the cases.[6]

Putting it all together, we have for the present value of a patent portfolio:

$$48. \quad PV(PP) = E \times \left[ 1 - \prod_{j=1}^{n}(1 - F_v^j) \right] \times \left[ 1 - \prod_{j=1}^{n}(1 - F_e^j) \right]$$

$$\times \left[ 1 - \prod_{j=1}^{n}(1 - F_i^j) \right] \times \sum_{i=1}^{I} \frac{\langle R \rangle_i \times \langle S \rangle_i - R_i \times S_i}{(1 + I_i)^i}$$

Or, in the simplified scenario of probabilities $F_i$, $F_v$, and $F_e$ fixed for all patents in the portfolio, we have

$$49. \quad PV(PP) = E \times \left[ 1 - (1 - F_e^j)^n \right] \times \left[ 1 - (1 - F_i^j)^n \right]$$

$$\times \left[ 1 - (1 - F_v^j)^n \right] \times \sum_{i=1}^{I} \frac{\langle R \rangle_i \times \langle S \rangle_i - R_i \times S_i}{(1 + I_i)^i}$$

To simplify it even further, we note that patentees prevail at trial in 58% of the cases.[7] More specifically, patentees prevail in 51% of the bench trials and in 68% of the jury trials.[8] Thus, we can significantly simplify expression (49) by replacing the probability of successful enforcement by this number:

$$50. \quad PV(PP) = E \times 0.58 \times \sum_{i=1}^{I} \frac{\langle R \rangle_i \times \langle S \rangle_i - R_i \times S_i}{(1 + I_i)^i}$$

Expression (50) gives a reasonably good estimate of patent portfolio value in general. Here, we make the assumption that we will one day have to defend our portfolio, but no infringement is known at the moment. Under this assumption, we can effectively manage the risk of infringement by purchasing two patent insurance policies: (1) a patent validity policy, and (2) an infringement abatement policy. The availability of these policies allows us to simplify the valuation analysis. We can now assume that one is determined to enforce one's patents ($E_w = 1$), and we can eliminate the probability factor $E_a$ ($E_a = 1$) and, instead, subtract the cost of the infringement abatement policy from the value of the patent portfolio. Similarly, probabilities $F_v$ and $F_e$ that the patent(s) will be found valid and enforceable can be now eliminated from the analysis and, instead, the cost of the patent validity insurance is subtracted. The only remaining unknown factor is the probability of finding infringement, $F_i$, which statistically is 66%. We can now rewrite expression (50) as

$$51. \quad PV(PP) = 0.66 \times \sum_{i=1}^{l} \frac{\langle R \rangle_i \times \langle S \rangle_i - R_i \times S_i}{(1 + I_i)^i} - A - B$$

where $A$ is the cost of the patent validity insurance policy and $B$ is the cost of the patent infringement abatement insurance policy. A patent validity policy insures only the patent for which it is purchased. For expression (50) to be valid, all patents in the portfolio must be insured. Assuming that $A^j$ is the cost of the validity policy for the patent $P^j$, we have

$$52. \quad PV(PP) = 0.66 \times \sum_{i=1}^{l} \frac{\langle R \rangle_i \times \langle S \rangle_i - R_i \times S_i}{(1 + I_i)^i} - \sum_{j=1}^{n} A^j - B$$

Since the cost of an insurance policy is primarily determined by the annual premiums, which we shall denote as $A_i^j$ and $B_i$, respectively, we will rewrite expression (52) as

$$53.\ PV(PP) = 0.66 \times \sum_{i=1}^{l} \frac{\langle R \rangle_i \times \langle S \rangle_i - R_i \times S_i}{(1 + I_i)^i} - \sum_{i=1}^{l} \sum_{j=1}^{n} A_i^j - \sum_{i=1}^{l} B_i$$

or

$$54.\ PV(PP) = 0.66 \times \sum_{i=1}^{l} \left[ \frac{\langle R \rangle_i \times \langle S \rangle_i - R_i \times S_i}{(1 + I_i)^i} - \sum_{j=1}^{n} A_i^j - B_i \right]$$

and

$$55.\ V(PP) = 0.66 \times \sum_{i=1}^{l} \left[ \left( \langle R \rangle_i \times \langle S \rangle_i - R_i \times S_i \right) - \sum_{j=1}^{n} A_i^j - B_i \right]$$

## Portfolio Net Present Value and Yield (IRR)

Let us now consider an important economic indicator of a patent portfolio: its yield or internal rate of return (IRR).

It is well known that the yield, or IRR, on an investment that produces annual cash flow $C_i$, is the interest rate that satisfies the equation

$$56.\ p = \sum_{i=1}^{n} \frac{C}{(1 + y)^i}$$

where $p$ is the price paid (or investment made); $C_i$ is the annual cash flow, $y$ is the yield, and $n$ is the number of years. Yield is determined by trial and error procedure.

In the case of a patent portfolio, the cash flow $C_i$ is equivalent to the annual value of the public franchise secured by the portfolio:

$$57.\ C_i = E \times \left[ 1 - \prod_{j=1}^{n}(1 - F_v^j) \right] \times \left[ 1 - \prod_{j=1}^{n}(1 - F_e^j) \right]$$

$$\times \left[ 1 - \prod_{j=1}^{n}(1 - F_i^j) \right] \times \left( \langle R \rangle_i \times \langle S \rangle_i - R_i \times S_i \right)$$

or, in the simplified scenario of probabilities $F_i$, $F_v$, and $F_e$ fixed for all patents in the portfolio, we have

$$58. \quad C_i = E \times \left[ 1 - (1 - F_e^j)^n \right] \times \left[ 1 - (1 - F_i^j)^n \right]$$

$$\times \left[ 1 - F_v^j)^n \right] \times \left( \langle R \rangle_i \times \langle S \rangle_i - R_i \times S_i \right)$$

or, with the validity and infringement abatement insurances in place, we have

$$59. \quad C_i = 0.66 \times \left[ \left( \langle R \rangle_i \times \langle S \rangle_i - R_i \times S_i \right) - \sum_{j=1}^{n} A_i^j - B_i \right]$$

Let us turn our attention now to the price (or investment), $p$. Traditionally, the cost of a patent, $p$, is thought to be the sum of the cost of prosecution (including the costs of drafting and filing the application), $p_p$, and the cost of maintenance (including payment of USPTO filing and issue fees), $p_m$:

$$60. \quad p = p_p + p_m$$

These numbers are well known. The cost of patent prosecution is between \$5,000 and \$19,000. Over the life of a patent, the minimum filing, issue, and maintenance fees are \$7,740 for a so-called large entity U.S. patent, and \$3,870 for a small entity U.S. patent.

However, it is a mistake to think that the cost of a patent is simply the cost of patent prosecution and maintenance. The true price paid for a patent includes disclosure of the invention. An inventor has a choice: Keep the invention secret, or disclose it in the hopes of obtaining a patent. An undisclosed invention, if kept confidential, is intellectual property too, protected as a trade secret.

Valuation techniques for trade secrets lay outside the scope of this appendix. What is important for our present discussion is understanding that the value of the trade secret is a part of the price paid for obtaining a patent. Thus, we are going to rewrite (60) as

$$61. \quad p = PV(TS) + p_p + p_m$$

where $PV(TS)$ is the present value of the trade secrets $TS$, forfeited in exchange for the constituent patents of the portfolio. Equation (56) now takes the form

$$62. \quad PV(TS) + p_p + p_m = \sum_{i=1}^{n} \frac{C_i}{(1 + y)^i}$$

The interest rate $y$ that satisfies this equation gives us the yield or the IRR of the patent portfolio.

## Value in the Event of a Known Infringement

When patent infringement occurs, the public franchise is violated, and the methodology developed above is no longer applicable. In this event, a patent or patent portfolio may only be worth as much as one expects to recover in damages through litigation (less the cost of litigation).

Any patent owner whose patents have been infringed and whose public franchise afforded by these patents has been compromised, would seek (aside from damages) a permanent injunction to restore the monopoly. Thus, the value of the patent portfolio is

$$23. \quad V(PP) = E \times F \times \sum_i \left( \langle R \rangle_i \times \langle S \rangle_i - R_i \times S_i \right) - C$$

where $C$ is the cost of patent litigation necessary to restore and enforce the public franchise.

The cost of litigation may be forecasted based on well-known statistics. According to the AIPLA 2000 survey, the median cost of patent litigation in the U.S. is 2 million dollars. Such statistics are available by state as well.

# Endnotes

[1]Assuming that this product or process does not infringe the patents of others.

[2]Pursuant to the American Inventor's Protection Act of 1999, the patent application published after 18 months from the date of application filing will enjoy provisional rights as of the date of application publication.

[3]We assumed here that the incremental revenues $\Delta$ are received at the end of the annual period.

[4]This assumption may be refined by further breaking down the summation periods into semiannual, quarterly, and monthly periods.

[5]Kimberly A. Moore, "Judges, Juries, and Patent Cases—An Empirical Peek Inside the Black Box," *Michl. L. Rev.* 99 (2001).

[6]Ibid.

[7]Ibid.

[8]Ibid.

# Invention Disclosure Form

(1) Full name, address, and telephone number of each person who conceived the invention:

(2) General subject matter and purpose of the invention, including an explanation of the problem(s) to be solved and the deficiencies in the existing technology:

(3) A description of the invention, including, if available:
   a. Drawings, photographs, charts, test results, etc.
   b. Identification of each novel feature
   c. An explanation of how the novel features provide advantages over the existing technology
   d. A description of any presently contemplated modifications, alterations, improvements, or extensions of the invention

(4) A description of the closest known prior art (attach copies of prior art documents if available):

Attach additional, consecutively numbered pages as needed, each having the signatures of the inventors and witnesses as indicated below:

**Inventor Signature(s) and Date:**          **Read and Understood by Witnesses:**

_____  _____          _____  _____
                    Date          (                    )  Date

                                   _____  _____
                                   (                    )  Date

# License Agreements

This template can be used for either a running royalty agreement or a paid-up license agreement. Only Section 3, "Payments," will change depending on the type of agreement used.

## NONEXCLUSIVE LIMITED PATENT
## LICENSE AGREEMENT

**THIS AGREEMENT** (hereinafter referred to as the "Agreement") is made by and between Licensor Company (hereinafter referred to as "Licensor"), a _____ [form of organization] with principal offices at _____ , and _____ , a _____ corporation with principal offices at _____ (hereinafter referred to as "Licensee").

## WITNESSETH:

**WHEREAS,** Licensor is the owner of all right, title and interest in United States Patent Nos. _____ (which patents are hereinafter collectively referred to as the "Licensed Patents");

**WHEREAS,** Licensee is in the business of making and selling _____ , and desires to obtain a nonexclusive license to make, use, and sell products and to practice the inventions covered by the Licensed Patents;

**WHEREAS,** Licensee has made and sold certain _____ [if applicable];

**WHEREAS,** Licensee consents that the Licensed Patents are valid and enforceable [if applicable];

**WHEREAS,** Licensee consents that the Licensed Patents have been infringed by certain products made, sold and/or offered for sale by Licensee [if applicable];

**WHEREAS,** Licensor and Licensee desire to enter into a license agreement covering the Licensed Patents; and

**WHEREAS,** Licensor has the right to grant a nonexclusive license to Licensee under the Licensed Patents and is willing to do so on the terms and conditions recited in this Agreement.

**NOW, THEREFORE,** in consideration of the preceding and the mutual covenants recited below, and for other good and valuable consideration, receipt and sufficiency of which is hereby acknowledged, the parties agree as follows:

## 1. DEFINITIONS

1.1 **Licensed Patents.** "Licensed Patents" as used in this Agreement shall mean the _____ , collectively, and any patent issued in the future from any reissue, reexamination, divisional, continuation and/or continuation-in-part of the Licensed Patents, including any foreign counterpart thereof.

1.2 **Territory.** "Territory" as used in this Agreement shall mean the United States and its territories and possessions. [If foreign patents are licensed, include respective countries.]

1.3 **Effective Date.** "Effective Date" shall mean _____ , _____ .

1.4 **Term.** "Term" as used in this Agreement shall mean the period beginning on the Effective Date and ending with the expiration of the last to expire of the Licensed Patents or the termination of this Agreement, whichever occurs first. This Agreement shall, if not terminated sooner, terminate at the end of the Term.

1.5 **Licensed Product.** "Licensed Product" as used in this Agreement shall mean certain _____ made, used, imported, sold or offered for sale by Licensee, including, but not limited to: _____ .

1.6 **Past Products.** "Past Products" as used in this Agreement shall mean the Licensed Products made or sold by Licensee before the Effective Date of this Agreement.

## 2. LICENSE

2.1 **License Grant**. Subject to the terms and conditions of this Agreement and the due performance by Licensee of Licensee's obligations under this Agreement and in reliance on Licensee's representations and warranties set forth in this Agreement, Licensor hereby grants to Licensee a personal, nonexclusive, nontransferable limited license under the Licensed Patents for the Term in the Territory to make, use, import, offer to sell, and sell Licensed Products and Past Products, with no right to sublicense. This license shall not extend to any third party, subsidiary, division, or any entity acquired after the Effective Date.

2.2 **Basis**. The foregoing license is granted solely under the Licensed Patents. No license under any other patents or intellectual property of Licensor is granted, either expressly or by implication.

2.3 **Marking**. During the Term of this Agreement, Licensee shall affix to Licensed Products a statement in substantially the form: "U.S. Patent Nos. ＿＿＿＿＿＿＿＿＿＿＿＿ ." The Licensee shall provide Licensor with the samples of its Licensed Products evidencing proper marking as required hereunder. From time to time, and within a reasonable time after written notice from Licensor, Licensor shall have the right to inspect Licensee's Licensed Products to determine if Licensee is marking in accordance with this paragraph.

2.4 **Past Sales**. Subject to the terms and conditions of this Agreement and the due performance by Licensee of its obligation to make the payment required by Paragraph 3.1, Licensor hereby grants to Licensee a nonexclusive limited license under the Licensed Patents on all Past Products.

## 3. PAYMENTS [*For running royalty license agreement*]

3.1 **Past Products**. For the rights granted in this Agreement relating to Licensee's Past Products, Licensee shall pay Licensor a past license fee of ＿＿＿＿ percent ( ＿%) of Licensee's net sales (defined as gross sales less returns and allowances) for each Past Product sold during the last six years from the Effective Date hereof, which shall be due and payable immediately upon the Effective Date hereof.

3.2 **Running Royalty.**

    3.21 <u>Royalty Payment</u>. For the rights granted in this Agreement, and subject to Paragraphs 3.2.2 and 3.2.3 hereinbelow, Licensee shall pay Licensor a royalty of ___ percent ( __ %) of Licensee's selling price for each Licensed Product manufactured, used, or sold by Licensee in the Territory or imported by Licensee into the Territory.

    3.22 <u>Termination of Royalty on Invalidity or Unenforceability</u>. The royalty payments shall terminate if all of the Licensed Patents are held invalid or unenforceable. A Licensed Patent shall be deemed invalid or unenforceable under this Agreement if a court or tribunal of competent jurisdiction makes such a determination, and the determination becomes final in that it is not further reviewable through appeal or exhaustion of all permissible petitions or applications for rehearing or review.

3.3 **Accrual.** A running royalty as to a unit of Licensed Product shall accrue on the day the unit is shipped or invoiced to a Licensee customer, whichever occurs first.

3.4 **Payment.** All royalty payments to Licensor shall be made quarterly by Licensee, with the first quarter being defined as January 1 through March 31, the second quarter as April 1 through June 30, the third quarter as July 1 through September 30, and the fourth quarter as October 1 through December 31. Payment of royalties shall be made to Licensor not later than the thirtieth (30th) day (the "Due Date") after the end of the period to which the payment relates. Each royalty payment as defined hereinabove shall be subject to and be no less than a minimum royalty of _____ ($ _____ ) Dollars per quarter.

3.5 **Accounting Statements**. Licensee shall provide Licensor with a statement of royalties due Licensor under this Agreement quarterly (as that term is defined in Paragraph 3.4) on or before the Due Date, setting forth the amount due to Licensor for the period and, in reasonable detail, the factual basis for calculating the amount.

3.6 **Interest**. Subject to the limits imposed by any applicable usury law, interest shall accrue on payments made more than ten (10) days after they are due at the rate of _____ percent ( __%) per annum, compounded daily, from the due date until paid.

3.7 **Books and Records and Audit**. Licensee shall keep full, complete, and accurate books of account and records covering all transactions relating to this Agreement. Licensee shall preserve such books and records for a period of three (3) years after the Due Date to which the material relates. Acceptance by Licensor of an accounting statement or payment hereunder will not preclude Licensor from challenging or questioning the accuracy thereof. During the Term and for a period of one (1) year thereafter, Licensor may, upon reasonable notice in writing to Licensee, cause an independent audit to be made of the books and records of Licensee in order to verify the statements rendered under this Agreement, and prompt adjustment shall be made by the proper party to compensate for any errors disclosed by the audit. The audit shall be conducted only by an independent accountant during regular business hours and in a reasonable manner so as not to interfere with normal business activities. Audits shall be made hereunder no more frequently than annually. Before any audit may be conducted, the auditor must represent that the auditor's fee will in no manner be determined by the results of the audit and must agree to maintain the confidentiality of all confidential material to which the auditor is given access. Licensor will bear all expenses and fees of the audit, but if the audit reveals an underpayment for any quarter of more than five percent (5%), Licensee shall pay all such expenses and fees. Licensee shall provide samples of any new _____ , and/or a complete written description thereof, sufficient to enable Licensor to determine whether such product is covered by any of the claims of any of the Licensed Patents.

3.8 **Patent Validity and Infringement.** Licensee acknowledges and consents that the Licensed Patents are valid and enforceable. [*If applicable*: Licensee further acknowledges that the Licensed Products infringe the Licensed Patents. Licensee admits that it has been infringing the Licensed Patents and this infringement shall be cured by the License granted hereunder.]

3.9 **Nonaggression.** Licensee shall not at any time, directly or indirectly, oppose the grant of, nor dispute the validity or enforceability of, nor cooperate in any suit, claim, counterclaim or defense against any patent or claim included in the Licensed Patents.

3.10 **Confidentiality.** Licensor and Licensee acknowledge that the amount of Licensee's payments actually made to Licensor under this Agreement are confidential and proprietary information relating to this Agreement and the business of Licensor and Licensee. Accordingly, the parties agree that each of them shall keep that information confidential and shall not disclose it, or permit it to be disclosed, to any third party (other than to agents or representatives who need to know such information). Licensor shall have the right, however, to disclose that Licensor and Licensee have entered into this Agreement, the royalty rate(s) set forth in this Agreement, that Licensee is paying for Past Products, and that Licensee has consented to the validity, enforceability and infringement of the Licensed Patents.

**3. PAYMENTS** [*For paid-up license agreement*]

3.1 **Paid-up License.** For the rights granted in this Agreement Licensee shall unconditionally pay Licensor a one-time license fee of _____ and 00/100 Dollars ($_____.00), which shall be due immediately upon the Effective Date and payable within three (3) days of the Effective Date.

3.2 **Patent Validity and Infringement.** Licensee acknowledges and consents that the Licensed Patents are valid and enforceable. [*If applicable:* Licensee further acknowledges that the Licensed Products infringe the Licensed Patents. Licensee admits that it has been infringing the Licensed Patents and that this infringement shall be cured by the license granted hereunder.]

3.3 **Nonaggression.** Licensee shall not at any time, directly or indirectly, oppose the grant of, nor dispute the validity or enforceability of, nor cooperate in any suit, claim, counterclaim or defense against any patent or claim including in the Licensed Patents.

3.4 **Confidentiality.** Licensor and Licensee acknowledge that the amount of Licensee's payments actually made to Licensor under this

Agreement are confidential and proprietary information relating to this Agreement and the business of Licensor and Licensee. Accordingly, the parties agree that each of them shall keep that information confidential and shall not disclose it, or permit it to be disclosed, to any third party (other than to agents or representatives who need to know such information). Licensor shall have the right, however, to disclose that Licensor and Licensee have entered into this Agreement, the royalty rate(s) set forth in this Agreement, that Licensee is paying for Past Products, and that Licensee has consented to the validity, enforceability and infringement of the Licensed Patents.

## 4. INDEMNIFICATION

4.1 **Licensee Indemnification**. Licensee shall at all times during the term of this Agreement and thereafter, indemnify, defend and hold Licensor, its directors, officers, employees and affiliates, harmless against all claims, proceedings, demands and liabilities of any kind whatsoever, including legal expenses and reasonable attorneys' fees, arising out of the death of or injury to any person or out of any damage to property, or resulting from the production, manufacture, sale, use, lease, or advertisement of Licensed Products or Past Products or arising from any obligation of Licensee under this Agreement.

4.2 **Licensor Indemnification**. Licensor shall at all times during the term of this Agreement and thereafter, indemnify, defend and hold Licensee, its directors, officers, employees and affiliates, harmless against all claims, proceedings, demands and liabilities of any kind whatsoever, including legal expenses and reasonable attorneys' fees, arising out of any breach of any representation, warranty, or covenant expressly made by Licensor in this Agreement.

## 5. TERMINATION

5.1 **Termination by Licensor**. In addition to all other remedies Licensor may have, Licensor may terminate this Agreement and the licenses granted in this Agreement in the event that:
(a) Licensee defaults in its payment to Licensor and such default continues unremedied for a period of thirty (30) days after the Effective Date of this Agreement;

(b) Licensee fails to perform any material obligation, warranty, duty or responsibility or is in default with respect to any term or condition undertaken by Licensee hereunder, and such failure or default continues unremedied for a period of thirty (30) days after written notice thereof to Licensee by Licensor;

(c) Licensee is liquidated or dissolved;

(d) Any assignment is made of Licensee's business for the benefit of creditors;

(e) Licensee liquidates a substantial portion of its business or engages in a distress sale of substantially all of its assets;

(f) A receiver, or similar officer, is appointed to take charge of a substantial part of Licensee's assets;

(g) Licensee is unable to pay its debts as they mature; or

(h) Any petition in bankruptcy is filed by or against Licensee that remains undischarged for sixty (60) days.

5.2 **Termination by Licensee**. If all the Licensed Patents are determined to be invalid or unenforceable by any court or tribunal of competent jurisdiction, and the determination becomes final in that it is not further reviewable through appeal or exhaustion of all permissible petitions or applications for rehearing or review, Licensee may terminate this Agreement at will and shall have no further obligations hereunder.

5.3 **Effect of Termination**. After the termination of this Agreement, Licensee shall have no rights under the Licensed Patents.

5.4 **No Discharge on Termination**. No termination of this Agreement for any reason shall relieve or discharge either Licensor or Licensee from any duty, obligation, or liability that was accrued as of the date of the termination (including, without limitation, the obligation to indemnify or to pay any amounts owing as of the date of termination).

## 6. REPRESENTATIONS AND WARRANTIES OF LICENSOR

6.1 **Right to Grant License**. Licensor represents and warrants that Licensor has the right and authority to grant the licenses granted to Licensee in this Agreement and that this Agreement and the licenses granted in this Agreement do not and will not conflict with the terms of any agreement to which Licensor is a party.

6.2 **Disclaimers.** Except as otherwise expressly set forth in this Agreement, Licensor, its directors, officers, employees, and agents make no representations and extend no warranties of any kind, either express or implied. In particular, and without limitation, nothing in this Agreement shall be construed as:

(a) a warranty or representation by Licensor as to the validity or scope of the Licensed Patents;

(b) a warranty or representation by Licensor that anything made, used, sold or otherwise disposed of under any license granted in this Agreement is or will be free from infringement of patents of third parties;

(c) an obligation on the part of Licensor to bring or prosecute actions against third parties for infringement of the Licensed Patents or other proprietary rights;

(d) an obligation on the part of Licensor to furnish any manufacturing or technical information;

(e) the granting by implication, estoppel, or otherwise of any licenses or rights under patents other than the Licensed Patents; or

(f) the assumption by Licensor of any responsibilities whatever with respect to use, sale, or other disposition by Licensee or its vendees or transferees of Licensed Products.

6.3 **Limitation of Liability.** In no event shall Licensor, its directors, officers, employees and affiliates be liable for incidental or consequential damages of any kind, including economic damage or injury to property and lost profits, regardless of whether Licensor shall be advised, shall have other reason to know, or in fact shall know of the possibility.

## 7. REPRESENTATIONS AND WARRANTIES OF LICENSEE

Licensee represents and warrants that Licensee has the right and authority to enter into this Agreement and that this Agreement and the exercise of the licenses granted hereunder does not and will not conflict with the terms of any agreement to which Licensee is a party. Except as otherwise expressly set forth in this Agreement, Licensee, its directors, officers, employees, and agents make no representations and extend no warranties of any kind, either express or implied. In particular, and without limitation, nothing in this Agreement shall be construed as an obligation on the part of Licensee to furnish any manufacturing or technical information.

## 8. RELATIONSHIP OF THE PARTIES

Nothing in this Agreement will be construed to constitute the parties as partners or joint ventures or constitute either party as agent of the other, nor will any similar relationship be deemed to exist between them. Neither party shall hold itself out contrary to the terms of this paragraph and neither party shall become liable by reason of any representation, act, or omission of the other contrary to the provisions of this paragraph. This Agreement is not for the benefit of any third party and shall not be deemed to give any right or remedy to any such party, whether referred to in this Agreement or not.

## 9. ASSIGNMENT

9.1 **No Assignment**. This Agreement, the rights granted to Licensee, and the duties and obligations of Licensee are all personal to Licensee and Licensee agrees not to sell, assign, transfer, mortgage, pledge or hypothecate any such rights in whole or in part, or delegate any of its duties or obligations under this Agreement; nor shall any of Licensee's rights or duties be assigned, transferred, delegated by Licensee to any third party by operation of law. Any purported transfer, assignment or delegation in violation of the foregoing sentence shall be void and without effect, and this Agreement shall thereupon become terminable without further notice by Licensor. In the context of this provision, "assignment" shall include the transfer of substantially all of the assets of Licensee, or of a majority interest in the voting stock of Licensee, or the merger, consolidation or reorganization of Licensee with one or more third parties.

9.2 **Binding on Successors**. This Agreement will inure to the benefit of and be binding upon Licensor, its successors, and assigns.

## 10. DISPUTE RESOLUTION

10.1 **Arbitration of Royalty Disputes.**

(a) Any dispute between Licensor and Licensee concerning the amount of royalties payable to Licensor under this Agreement shall be submitted for binding arbitration in accordance with the provisions of this Section 10 and the then-applicable rules of the American Arbitration Association (the "Association"). Judgment upon the arbitration award may be entered in any court of competent jurisdiction.

(b) The power of the arbitrators shall be limited to resolving the specific issues stated by determining the royalties Licensee owes or should receive credit for, if any, under this Agreement. The power of the arbitrators shall not extend to any other matters. All other disputes shall be subject to litigation in a court of competent jurisdiction.

(c) The arbitration panel or tribunal shall consist solely of neutral arbitrators.

(d) The parties agree that arbitration proceedings under this Agreement shall not be stayed on the ground of pending litigation to which either or both of them is a party.

10.2 **Remedies**. Except as expressly provided herein, all specific remedies provided for in this Agreement are cumulative and are not exclusive of one another or of any other remedies available in law or equity.

## 11. LIMITATIONS OF RIGHTS AND AUTHORITY

11.1 **Limitation of Rights.** No right or title whatsoever in the Licensed Patents is granted by Licensor to Licensee, or shall be taken or assumed by Licensee, except as is specifically set forth in this Agreement.

11.2 **Limitation of Authority.** Neither party shall, in any respect whatsoever, be taken to be the agent or representative of the other party, and neither party shall have any authority to assume any obligation for the other party, or to commit the other party in any way.

## 12. MISCELLANEOUS

12.1 **Computation of Time.** The time in which any act provided in this Agreement is to be done shall be computed by excluding the first day and including the last day, unless the last day is a Saturday, Sunday, or legal holiday, and then it shall also be excluded.

12.2 **Notices.** All notices given in connection with this Agreement shall be in writing and shall be deemed given upon actual receipt by the addressee. Notices shall be personally delivered or sent by telex or facsimile (with prompt confirmation by registered or certified air mail, postage prepaid) or by registered or certified air mail, postage prepaid, addressed to the party to be notified at the following address, or at such other address as the party may designate by notice:

Licensor:

_____

_____

_____

Attention: _____

Phone: _____

Facsimile: _____

Licensee:

_____

_____

_____

Attention: _____

Phone: _____

Facsimile: _____

12.3 **Survival.** The provisions of this Agreement relating to payment obligations, confidentiality, indemnification, remedies, and arbitration shall survive the expiration or termination of this Agreement.

12.4 **Severability**. If any provision of this Agreement is declared by a court of competent jurisdiction to be invalid, illegal, unenforceable, or void then both parties shall be relieved of all obligations arising under such provision, but only to the extent that such provision is invalid, illegal, unenforceable, or void. If the remainder of this Agreement is capable of substantial performance, then each provision not so affected shall be enforced to the extent permitted by law.

12.5 **Waiver and Modification**. No modification of any of the terms of this Agreement will be valid unless in writing and signed by both parties. No waiver by either party of a breach of this Agreement will be deemed a waiver by such party of any subsequent breach.

12.6 **Headings**. The headings in this Agreement are for reference only and shall not in any way control the meaning or interpretation of this Agreement.

12.7 **Interpretation**. No provision of this Agreement is to be interpreted for or against any party because that party or its attorney drafted the provision.

12.8 **Governing Law**. This Agreement shall be construed, governed, interpreted, and applied in accordance with the laws of the State of _____.

12.9 **No Other Agreement**. The parties each represent that in entering into this Agreement, they rely on no promise, inducement, or other agreement not expressly contained in this Agreement; that they have read this Agreement and discussed it thoroughly with their respective legal counsel; that they understand all of the provisions of this Agreement and intend to be bound by them; and that they enter into this Agreement voluntarily.

12.10 **Entire Agreement**. This Agreement constitutes the complete and exclusive statement of the terms and conditions between the parties, which supersedes and merges all prior proposals, understandings and all other agreements, oral and written, between the parties relating to the subject of this Agreement.

12.11 **Counterparts**. This Agreement may be executed in counterparts, which taken together shall constitute one document.

**IN WITNESS WHEREOF**, the parties have executed this Agreement by their duly authorized representatives.

**For and on behalf of**

_____     Date: _____

By: _____

Title: _____


**For and on behalf of**
**[Licensee]**

_____     Date: _____

By: _____

Title: _____

# Bibliography

Moore, Kimberly A. "Judges, Juries, and Patent Cases—An Empirical Peek Inside the black Box." *Mich. L. Rev.* 99 (2001).

Quinn, Eugene R., Jr. "Using Alternative Dispute Resolution to Resolve Patent Litigation: A Survey of Patent Litigators." *3 Marquette Intell. Propl. L. Rev.* 77 (1999).

Smith, Gordon V. and Russell L. Parr. *Valuation of Intellectual Property and Intangible Assets.* New York: John Wiley & Sons, Inc., 1989.

Vermont, Samson. "Business Risk Analysis: The Economics of Patent Litigation." In *From Ideas to Assets: Investing Wisely in Intellectual Property,* edited by Bruce Berman. New York: John Wiley & Sons, Inc., 2001.

Stewart, Thomas A. *Intellectual Capital, the New Wealth of Organizations.* New York: Doubleday/Currency, 1997.

# Further Reading

Rivette, Kevin G. and David Kline. *Rembrandts in the Attic.* Boston: Harvard Business School Press, 2000.

Stewart, Thomas A. *Intellectual Capital, the New Wealth of Organizations.* New York: Doubleday/Currency, 1997.

Sullivan, Patrick H. *Profiting from Intellectual Capital, Extracting Value From Innovation.* New York: John Wiley & Sons, Inc., 1998.

Chisum, Donald S., Craig Allen Nard, Herbert F. Schwartz, Pauline Newman, and F. Scott Kieff. *Principles of Patent Law.* New York: Foundation Press, 1998.

Davis, Julie L. and Suzanne S. Harrison. *Edison in the Boardroom.* New York: John Wiley & Sons, Inc., 2000.

Shulman, Seth. *Owning the Future.* New York: Houghton Mifflin, 1999.

Berman, Bruce, ed. *From Ideas to Assets: Investing Wisely in Intellectual Property.* New York: John Wiley & Sons, Inc., 2001.

Smith, Gordon V. and Russell L. Parr. *Valuation of Intellectual Property and Intangible Assets.* New York: John Wiley & Sons, Inc., 1989.

# Index